DIGITAL NOMAD

AUTHOR'S NOTE

Times are changing. The driving force of change in the world is technological advance. It has forced companies to downsize, merge, de-merge and acquire to obtain the capabilities they think are needed.

The change is invisible, unstoppable and accelerating. It is pushing in two directions: towards smaller, cheaper, more portable personal tools, and towards the imminence of cheap, high capacity, global communications networks.

Technology does not cause change but it amplifies change. Early in the next millennium it will deliver the capability to live and work on the move.

The world's major technology companies are targeting the lifestyle of the 'mobile professional' in developing the tools for leading a nomadic business life. In time these tools will become cheap enough for everyone, and the biggest lifestyle change for 10,000 years – since humans stopped being nomadic and settled down to farm – will be delivered to most people in the developed world.

People will therefore be able to ask themselves, 'Am I a nomad or a settler?' For the first time in 10,000 years that choice will become a mainstream life-style option. This is the message of DIGITAL NOMAD.

DIGITAL NOMAD

Tsugio Makimoto & David Manners

JOHN WILEY & SONS

Chichester · New York · Weinheim · Brisbane · Singapore · Toronto

Other Wiley Editorial Offices

John Wiley & Sons, Inc., 605 Third Avenue,
New York, NY 10158-0012, USA

VCH Verlagsgesellschaft, Pappelallee 3, 0-69469
Weinheim, Germany

Jacaranda Wiley Ltd, 33 Park Road, Milton,
Queensland 4064, Australia

John Wiley & Sons (Asia) Pte Ltd, 2 Clementi Loop #02-01,
Jin Xing Distripark, Singapore 129809

John Wiley & Sons (Canada) Ltd, 22 Worcester Road,
Rexdale, Ontario M9W 1L1, Canada

Library of Congress Cataloging-in-Publication Data

British Library Cataloguing in Publication Data

A catalogue record for this book is available from the British Library

ISBN 0-471-97499-4

Typeset in 11/17pt Garamond by Dorwyn Ltd, Rowlands Castle, Hants
Printed and bound in Great Britain by Biddles Ltd, Guildford and King's Lynn
This book is printed on acid-free paper responsibly manufactured from
sustainable forestation, for which at least two trees are planted for each one
used for paper production.

For
Toshiki, Sasha, Yoshiko, Gemma, Nobuo and Akio

CONTENTS

ILLUSTRATIONS

ACKNOWLEDGMENTS

The authors express their particular thanks to Mitsugu Yoneyama without whose invaluable help this book could not have been completed.

We would also like to thank Toshimasa Kihara, Hajime Yasuda, Kazuo Minorikawa, Dr Eiji Takeda, Masashi Kazama, Steve Dow, Matthew Trowbridge, Richard Wilson, Steve Bush, Dr Roy Rubenstein, Richard Ball, Leon Clifford and David Lawrence for their ideas and contributions, and Scott and Denise Marshall at whose villa near Seillans in the south of France some of the ideas in this book were first discussed.

THE NOMADIC OPPORTUNITY

'Man started out as nomadic, it may be the
most natural state for human beings.'
Craig O. McCaw, McCaw Cellular

J UNE 21st 1995. If a date is needed for the start of the New
Nomadic Age, this is as good as any. Late that afternoon, at
Hakodate in Japan, Flight No. ANA857 was stalled on the local
airport runway. The reason—a hijack.

In the following 16 hours, twelve phone calls from passengers using
their mobile phones told police that the hijacker was aged 22–30, that
he wore sunglasses, jeans and white sneakers, that he was on the
upper floor of the aircraft and that he appeared to be lightly armed.

Acting on this information, police stormed the plane and arrested the hijacker without ill-effects except that a stewardess was slightly injured and one of the passengers, pop singer Tokiko Kato, complained of being 'worn out and wanting to sleep'.

There could be no better example of the power of one of the early tools of the New Nomadic Age—the mobile telephone—to alter events. The phone is just the start of it. Over the next decade technology will deliver to us a range of tools that will give us all the facilities of our homes and offices—in our pockets.

That will make each of us very powerful because it will make us geographically independent of our homes and offices. It will also give us a difficult personal choice. Do we stay put or do we roam? Are we settlers or nomads?

Wanderlust is part of the human psyche. Sociologists may attribute it to urges inherited from nomadic ancestors; psychologists may attribute it to human curiosity; cynics put it down to escapism; but wherever it comes from, the travel bug seems to grab us when it gets the opportunity.

Most of us, most of the time, don't have much opportunity to travel. We have jobs to hold down and households to maintain. Ever since most humans relinquished the nomadic lifestyle for the settled existence of farming—some 10,000 years ago—most of us have been economically tied to a geographic area.

But not for much longer. Within the next decade, for the first time for 10,000 years, most people will find that the geographic tie is dissolving. It will happen gradually and people will be slow to realise that a revolution is occurring but, by the end of those ten years, most people in the developed world will find themselves free to live where they want and travel as much as they want.

The 21st century will be the millennium which resurrects for humans a dilemma which has been dormant for 10,000 years—humans will be able to ask themselves: 'Am I a Nomad or a Settler?'.

Trying to predict human behaviour in new circumstances is usually a waste of time. However, the past can give clues to the future and the inescapable fact is that, despite 10,000 years of settled existence being the mainstream lifestyle on this planet, and despite determined efforts by governments around the world to discourage nomadic lifestyles, in some places the old nomadic way of life has remained intact.

Something remains, it seems, of the instincts which drove humans for two million years to be nomadic hunter-gatherers before they settled down—only 10,000 years ago—to farm.

For instance, the Bedouin still roam over vast areas of desert in the Sahara, Arabia, Iraq, Syria and Jordan. They despise agricultural work and manual labour and regard those who perform such work as an inferior life-form.

The Bedouin lead a predictable nomadic existence, herding their animals—camels, sheep and goats—into the desert during the rainy winter season and back towards more cultivated regions in the heat and aridity of the summer. They do not accumulate possessions (too heavy) and regard hurrying as the devil's work (too hot), and they have retained their way of life despite years of efforts by governments to settle them down.

Governments naturally hate nomads. They are difficult to tax and impossible to control. Therefore to governments they have traditionally represented a threat. The 1980s surge of the 'New Age Travellers' in the UK—groups of mainly automobile-based travellers—riled the British government sufficiently to provoke them into passing legislation to restrict the travellers' activities.

In Mongolia, the government has tried for generations to settle groups of wandering Mongols who live in collapsible tents called ger or yurts and wander from pasture to pasture. Their ancestors, some 20,000 to 35,000 years ago, are thought to have wandered into Alaska looking for food and became the first human inhabitants of the Americas. It is thought that it took them until 6,000–10,000BC to roam all the way down to Tierra del Fuego at the southernmost end of the South American continent.

The Mongols' descendants, the Red Indians of North America, led nomadic lifestyles until comparatively recently. For instance, the Sioux wandered the Great Plains of North America hunting wild animals until military defeats in the 1870s led to their being herded, with other formerly nomadic tribes, into reservations. The Red Indian 'Ghost Dance' religion preaches a coming of a messiah who will lead them back to the old nomadic ways.

To the present day, the famous Bushmen of Africa's Kalahari desert—the 'Kalahari-san'—practise the same hunter-gatherer nomadic lifestyle they have followed for 20,000 years, though these days they rely mostly on herding cattle.

In West Africa the Fulani nomads still wander with their cattle though the grasslands of Niger, and in Kenya the Masai also pursue pastoral nomadism, wandering well-known routes to find pasture for their cows, goats and sheep.

Some Aborigines in Australia still practise a nomadic lifestyle in the desert where they were driven by the European settlers who expelled them from their traditional hunting grounds.

Other nomads wander to practise their professions, such as the Lohar blacksmiths of India and, most numerous of all nomads, the ubiquitous gypsies who traditionally trade animals, repair metal goods, play music, tell fortunes, provide entertainment and beg.

Governments are routinely hostile to gypsies. The Nazis put them in concentration camps; the French have passed laws forbidding them to have campsites; while under Communism, eastern bloc European countries tried to stop their migratory ways by forcing them into settlements.

Despite the antagonism of governments and the general population's suspicion of gypsies, there remain, it is estimated, up to six million gypsies in the world—a considerable tribute to the satisfactions of nomadism.

These hardy, surviving, modern-day examples of nomadism suggest that it may not be too fanciful to assume that an urge to wander still beats in the human breast and, given the right economic conditions and incentives, could become so encouraged that nomadism re-establishes itself as a mainstream lifestyle.

The forces that are unleashing the ties of geography for people are the unstoppable forces of technological evolution. These are delivering increasingly inexpensive and efficient means of communicating with family and friends, office and customers, libraries and information sources of every kind.

At the moment, we do not have the ability to communicate by video link between any two points on the planet. But we will have it, and it will be generally affordable, within ten years. We will be able to see people, documents and pictures wherever they happen to be, from anywhere we happen to be.

That is the nature of the revolution which is going to give people options on a scale never seen before. With the ability to tap into every worldwide public information source from anywhere on the globe, and the ability to talk to anyone via a video link, humans are going to be given the opportunity, if they want it, of being global nomads.

Will they want to be? 'No', say most of us. We think of ourselves as settled. It is part of the mainstream lifestyle not only to be settled in one spot but to think we like it. 'There's no place like home', we tell ourselves; 'home is where the heart is'. Gardens, neighbours, schools, friends, family, job—all tie us to a neighbourhood.

Ten millennia of settled existence have made most of us think of ourselves as static creatures, of fixed address and office. We tend to define ourselves by our house and our job. The type of house we live in, where that house is, the car we drive and the type of job we do are all linked to our self-image and to how we think others see us.

As things are, in most of the developed world all these defining elements in our lives are related to a particular geographical spot on the planet. Once away from that spot we feel less certain of ourselves. Home is a more comfortable place to be.

With most of us feeling that we are settled, home-loving beings, it is really quite extraordinary that whenever technology has come along to allow us to travel more freely, we have eagerly embraced it. Sometimes we have changed our lives drastically to take advantage of the new opportunities.

For instance, when the technology of the steam train became widely available, it was wildly popular. Railway companies proliferated and speculation in the shares of new railway companies became rife. Many people went bust but the popularity of the new means of transport was great among ordinary people whose only means of long-distance transport had been horse-drawn or by boat.

Much of the initial popularity of the railway among ordinary people was not for its utilitarian side but as a diversion. People simply enjoyed the experience of going somewhere—going to the seaside or to the mountains or to visit another town or village. However, it was not long before people came to see the railways as a way to permanently change their lifestyle.

People realised that the railways would allow them to live away from the area where their workplace was located. Since workplaces tended to be in grimy industrial cities, it was attractive to many to move out to live and to travel into work every day on the train. So suburbia was spawned and the commuter was born.

From being geographically tied to one limited area, around the workplace, people were liberated by the train to extend their territorial ties to two places—the workplace and the home. Humans became daily travellers, some routinely commuting for four, five, even six hours a day.

Automobile technology made commuting all the easier and all the more widespread. If a man from Mars was looking down on our planet, he would see, as the Sun came up across the developed parts of Earth illuminating each time zone in its turn, a series of scurries of activity breaking out as each time zone arrived at 7:30 am.

The Martian would see an hour and a half of frenetic movements as humans leave their houses and walk, drive cars or take trains to their workplaces. For instance, 300,000 people travel into London every workday morning.

From 5 pm in each time zone, as the sunlight weakened or disappeared, he would witness another hour or two of serial scurries back from work to home. Truly, he might conclude, these creatures are obsessed with travelling.

Of course, if the Martian could look into the hearts and minds of the commuters, he would see that they were not necessarily travelling out of any intrinsic urge to travel—far from it!—but we are, to an extent, routinely nomadic.

If the Martian watched for longer than just the commuting hours, he would see a constant and growing stream of aeroplanes flying around the world. At any one time it is estimated that there are 300,000 people in aeroplanes flying over the US—a permanent flying city.

In 1995, IATA estimated that its affiliated airlines carried 1.2 billion passengers, which means that three and a half million people fly somewhere every day on a scheduled flight—and that doesn't take into account the millions flying on charter flights. IATA reckons that the number of scheduled flight passenger journeys is growing by 5–6% worldwide every year.

In fast-growing Asia the situation is much more dramatic, with air traffic expected to grow by closer to 20% a year. Over 50 new Asian airlines have been established during the past five years.

No wonder the world has ever-expanding airports (notably Narita, Heathrow, Manchester, Frankfurt, Dallas/Fort Worth), and a string of new airports either built or under construction: Hong Kong, Inchon in Korea, Munich, Kansai at Osaka in Japan, Kuala Lumpur, Shanghai and Haikou. In 1995, mainland China completed nine major airport construction or expansion projects, with another eight completed in 1996.

The world's busiest airport, Heathrow, handles over 400,000 take-offs and landings every year. No sooner did it open a new terminal, Terminal 4, than it was applying for permission to build Terminal 5.

In terms of numbers of passengers, air travel pales into insignificance beside rail travel. The railways in India carry four billion people a year and railways in China carry over one billion—but they are peanuts compared to Japan where just one railway company out of many, the East Japan Railway, carries six billion people a year. The West Japan Railway carries 1.8 billion a year, and there are a number of other railways in Japan which each carry over half a billion passengers a year.

Our Martian would also notice the constant construction of new hotels to service all these travellers. Every year over half a million new hotel rooms are built to add to the worldwide total of over 23 million rooms. Amazingly, over 80% of those hotel rooms are in Europe and America, yet the fastest growing travel destination is Asia. In Asia, the hotel building boom is explosive—adding 11% more hotel rooms every year—with a long way to go to catch up Europe and the US.

Our Martian would also see the ever-expanding production of automobiles. According to the World Automotive Trade Statistics compiled by the Society of Motor Manufacturers and Traders, over 30 million new automobiles are produced every year to add to a worldwide total of over 600 million vehicles in use on the planet—one for every 8.6 people on Earth. When the proportion of car-owners in mainland China rises from 1% of the population to 5%—as it certainly will—the annual car market will more than double!

The technology of the jet engine has transformed the lives of the student, the businessman and the retired, though not perhaps the group of international socialites who took their name from it—the Jet Set. The rich had always been great travellers long before the jet engine came along.

Historically, the rich have roamed the globe from pleasure ground to pleasure ground and from one fashionable event to the next. Without economic constraints or work responsibilities, many appear to find diversion in the stimulus of constant change.

Today, the rich happily travel from Melbourne in Australia, to Ascot and Cheltenham in England, to Longchamps in France, to Dublin in Ireland to watch horse racing; they will travel from Newport, Rhode Island, to Sydney in Australia, to Cowes in the Isle of Wight to watch yacht racing; and from Monte Carlo to Indianapolis to England's Brands Hatch to France's Le Mans to watch car racing.

As incomes for working people increase, they also increase their pleasure travel. Working people in Europe routinely take two or three foreign holidays a year, and in Germany it is often more.

All of this suggests that the urge to travel is strong within many of us and, given the freedom and the money to do it, we'll enthusiastically embark upon it.

Apart from the rich, there's another group who demonstrate that the nomadic urge beats strong in the human breast—the ex-repressed. In the countries of the former eastern bloc and in China, people have for decades been forcibly deprived of the right to travel. But now, once they have passed the economic stages of finding they can buy new clothes, consumer durables, cars and apartments the next thing they want to spend their money on is travel.

With more and more of the 450 million citizens of the former eastern European bloc, plus some of the billion citizens of China, finding travel affordable in the coming years, the surge of humanity taking to the world's travelling routes is unquenchable.

And as incomes in the developed and developing world rise, so the relative costs of travel are inexorably falling. Thanks to the jet engine and the jumbo, international travel has for many years been available to the masses and not just to the privileged few. As the planes get bigger, the fares get smaller. The next generation of jumbos could carry up to 1,000 passengers which could slash current fare levels and further stimulate demand.

For the developed world, the cost of travel is already no longer an issue which dissuades many people from travelling. Indeed, it has been estimated that the average American is prepared to spend as much on travel as he or she does on food.

Those in the developed world who have the freedom to travel, such as students and the retired, are increasingly on the move. In some cases, the retired find it cheaper to travel than to stay at home, because a pension earned by working in the developed world may not seem very generous when spent at home but can provide a very comfortable existence when spent in the developing or under-developed world. Pensioners might baulk at the thought of travelling in Iraq but, with the average mid-1990s Iraqi monthly wage worth $1.30, a typical Western pension would fund a princely lifestyle!

It is not uncommon to find tour companies offering six-month-long vacations which are clearly aimed at the retired, and if it is possible to rent out your house while you are travelling—as people increasingly do—then a pensioner might find that six months' travelling would earn him a nice profit.

For the student, travelling is more truly nomadic than for the retired. Where the retired tend to settle in hotels for days or even weeks at a time, the student backpackers carry their shelter and clothes on their backs and travel almost incessantly. They tend to roam whole regions—Europe, North America, South-East Asia—rather than visit single countries. Armed with cheap Euro-Rail passes they 'do' Europe; with cheap standby air tickets allowing 20 or so internal flights for a single, fairly modest, payment they cross and re-cross North America; with backpacks and rail tickets they roam through South-East Asia.

Just as the nomads of a million years ago wandered looking for animals to hunt or pastures to graze, modern-day backpackers wander in search of new places which stimulate their intellects and their senses. Having found them, and reaped enjoyment from them, they move on to find new stimulations and satisfactions. It's an improved, modern form of nomadism—cerebral nomadism instead of Stone Age hunter-gatherer nomadism.

So, where the freedom to roam exists—and the retired and the young have that freedom—roaming is very much on the increase.

That is a tribute to the pleasures of nomadism but it could also be an answer to one of the most intractable problems of modern life—unemployment.

With 19 million unemployed people in Western Europe alone, it is becoming a threat to social stability to have people cut off from society but continuing to live within it. The rising crime rates in the West show how unstable this situation is becoming. However, with travel and accommodation in the less developed world very much less expensive than in the developed world, we could convert this problem into an opportunity for the unemployed to find pleasurable change and recreation.

We have not yet got to the point where the average Western welfare cheque will subsidise a life of travel, but maybe it is not over-fanciful to see it becoming possible in the next century.

Renewable energy resources such as solar power that are scarce in the industrialised northern hemisphere are more abundant in the south, where solar-powered tourist resorts are economically viable. Staffed and supplied by the local population, these cities could contribute handsomely to the local economy and, where necessary, the food and wine surpluses of the developed world could be delivered to supplement local resources. These leisure cities could accommodate, very affordably, the unemployed of the developed world and give them a more enjoyable lifestyle than many of them currently enjoy.

Of course, there is the danger of such cities becoming invaded by everyone from the developed world seeking a Shangri-La opt-out from the pressures of modern life! But that is a problem for the politicians and the employers, who should be looking to create sufficiently satisfying working lives for their people for them not to seek a Shangri-La.

So, nomadism appears to be providing satisfaction for those who have the freedom to enjoy it, but what of the people who do not have nomadic freedoms? This is where the new wave of technology is going to make the most difference.

For many businesspeople, for whom a nomadic lifestyle is an enforced and much regretted here-and-now necessity, the arrival of new technologies will give more control over their travel schedules.

How often we see businesspeople who have arranged, some weeks before they set off, every detail of a multi-country travel schedule—every flight, every car journey, every hotel, the time of every meeting. All have been set down in stone, and so tight are some of these arrangements that to miss a connection is to jeopardise the remainder of their trip. This is Nomadism from Hell!

However, armed with video links to every part of his business and to every one of his customers and suppliers—on a screen big enough to exchange and amend documents while linked up to several people at once—a businessman might gain some relief from an inflexible, boss-imposed itinerary.

With a link into the Internet, anyone can already access exactly the same information as a travel agent. Once his links are truly portable, allowing access to any travel information source on the globe, the New Age Businessman will be liberated from an inconvenient itinerary by being able to rearrange his travel schedule 'on the fly'.

Finding himself in a pleasant part of the world and enabled by technology to run his business from a hotel room (or even a beach) without being at the mercy of the latest crisis call, he can take time out to enjoy himself free from the dictates of a rigid travel schedule set by a zealous secretary or a demanding boss.

Of course, for some workers—those tied to a production line in a factory, or to a particular person, like a secretary—there will not be any benefit to be gained from the new technologies. For them the new technologies might even make things worse, with 'the boss' frequently using electronic links to check up on the secretary's day-to-day activities instead of allowing the secretary a quiet few days in their absence.

For shop, restaurant, garage and hotel workers and all who need to be in a physical location to do their job, the new technological capabilities don't seem to offer much, although it is becoming easier for them to do those kinds of jobs wherever in the world they wish to go.

But for a sharply increasing number of workers—those who are selling individual skills—the new wave of technology will have a big impact because it will make them location-independent.

If a job does not require you to meet a supervisor face-to-face, or personally to visit materials suppliers or customers or regularly attend a physical location, the new capabilities will allow you to travel freely and carry on working.

In the so-called 'information age' this will apply to more and more workers. People whose function is the processing of information in one form or another—graphic artists, writers, designers, software writers and the like—are going to be more and more the mainstream type of worker in the next century.

So for anyone who can obtain the information they need to do their job down a telephone line or over a radio or video link, and who can deliver their work in the same way, nomadism will be a lifestyle option.

There is one group of people for whom the nomadic lifestyle does not seem to loom—parents. Schools are a geographic tie from which it seems impossible to break free. But even here there is a major shift from personal teaching to electronic teaching. Modern-day students are encouraged to use computers to access information. More and more information is available in the very portable form of a CD-ROM, one of which will hold an entire encyclopaedia, and a set of which would allow students to carry around with them an entire copy of the sources for their coursework.

Added to that will be 'narrow-casting'. As the cost of telecommunications time tumbles, it will become cost-effective to watch a lecture or a demonstration or engage in a class discussion via a video link—this is what is called 'narrow-casting.' By using it, a student will be able to join his or her classmates by video link when it is inconvenient to be there in person.

University courses in the 21st century may well routinely include lectures by eminent academics in other countries which are 'narrow-cast' to those students wanting to see them. Universities could become 'virtual', setting courses and conferring degrees without the physical manifestations of buildings or campus.

In the UK there has been such a university since the 1970s—the 'Open University'—which uses television for lectures and the postal service for teacher–student interaction. The new technologies coming along will add to that formula the narrow-casting of lectures and real-time student–teacher–classroom discussion from anywhere in the world to anywhere a student happens to be.

So, for the student, the retired, the businessperson, the information worker and even the unemployed, the delights of nomadism beckon. But will they want it? Given all the technological possibilities that the next decade will bring, will people grab them as an opportunity to become nomadic, or will they see them as an opportunity to become totally static?

The technology, of course, affords both possibilities. It can create the ultimate 'couch potato', someone who never leaves the living-room sofa, or the ultimate nomad, someone who is forever on the move. But all that the technology will do is provide the choices. Humans will decide which they want to make.

What needs to happen before that becomes possible? There are three requirements: first, the urge to travel coupled with the freedom to do it; second, an affordable, portable piece of equipment providing two-way mobile video links and access to every conceivable information source; and third, inexpensive communications links.

There is good news about the second and third of these requirements. 'The history of the 1980s was free MIPS', says Dr Andrew S. Grove, President of Intel, the world's biggest microchip firm; 'the history of the 1990s will be free bauds'. MIPS is the measure of the performance of a computer (millions of instructions per second); bauds is the measure of the performance of a communications link (the number of units of information that can be sent down it in one second).

With virtually free computing and free communications we have the basis for the Complete Nomadic Toolset. Why does the nomad need computing power? Because only computing power will do all that is required, for example to store information, to search other computers for more information, to draw pictures, charts and write text, to receive broadcasts and narrowcasts, to communicate via wires and radio, to display information on a screen, to receive and transmit video, documents and photos, and to print out hard copy.

All that takes up a lot of computing power—the power of a PC plus that of a workstation, a TV, a camcorder, a fax, and telephones, both mobile and conventional. The process of merging these types of equipment is already under way. Combined PC/TVs are on the market; combined printer/faxes are also being sold today.

To be affordable and useful, this Complete Nomadic Toolset has to weigh not much more than two pounds, cost the consumer about $500, ¥56000, £300 or DM750, and be as portable as a book. That's a tall order to complete between now and 2000 if you look at the size and cost of the equipment that performs all those functions today.

Is it possible? Well, let's assume that the computing power required is 250 MIPS—as powerful as the 1996 Pentium Pro from Intel and comparable with the 1997 300 MIPS SH4 from Hitachi. When Dr Grove says that MIPS are free, he's not saying *lots* of MIPS are free; what he means is that one MIPS is now almost free.

In the last ten years, the cost per MIPS of a microprocessor has come down by two orders of magnitude—from over $100 to $1 or

$2. By the early 21st century we can expect that the cost per MIPS will be down to around $0.1. This means that the processor cost for the Complete Nomadic Toolset will be around $25 in the early 21st century. As well as the processor, the toolset will need memory chips and control chips, making up a total chip cost of $100.

Today the cost of the chips represents 10–20% of an electronic product's total cost. This percentage is increasing. So, if we imagine ourselves in the 21st century setting off to purchase a 250 MIPS Complete Nomadic Toolset, we can expect to be paying $500.

However, if the way in which pocket telephones were marketed and popularised is anything to go by, the network operators will offer big discounts on the equipment to get consumers to sign up to their networks.

Bearing in mind that, by the end of the century, the networks will be global and therefore will be offering huge potential returns to their operators, it is likely that there could be a substantial element of subsidy to bring the price to the consumer down to affordable levels very quickly indeed.

As to size of the equipment, the trend is that the volume of the equipment involved—computers, camcorders, TVs, phones, faxes, etc.—is decreasing by one order of magnitude every ten years. That rate of progress should reduce the current collective size of all those machines to the point where, by 2000, they should be as portable as a hardback book.

So much for the equipment of nomadism. More unpredictable is the cost of the communications links. Here lies a consumer horror story.

Ever since the invention of the telephone 120 years ago, the telephone user has been shamelessly exploited. The universal reaction of governments throughout the world to the setting up of telephone networks was to nationalise them and hold them as a state monopoly.

Prices could be fixed at whatever level the monopoly decided. Some monopolies insisted on renting, rather than selling, telephones. All the monopolies required users to pay a regular fixed fee, even if the service was not used, just for the privilege of being allowed to use it.

Suppliers of equipment were loftily told what was required. Competition among suppliers was usually restricted to the domestic market. Not surprisingly, technological progress was pedestrian, innovation was rare, and prices were high.

This conspiracy against the consumer went unchecked for around 100 years until, in the last 30 years of the 20th century, governments decided that here was a potentially high-growth industrial sector whose sleepy ways were inappropriate to free-market economies.

The dreaded word for the monopolies was 'Deregulation'. Just as terrifying for them were 'Competition' and 'Market Forces'. For the telephone industry it was a whole new ball game.

For the consumer, however, there was a gradual realisation that things could get better. He could buy a phone and not have to keep paying rent for one; there was the opportunity to switch to a new network operator who charged less; free competition among equipment suppliers meant a host of competitively priced new goods—answerphones, cordless phones, fax machines, etc.—appearing in the shops.

In the USA, local calls became free. In some parts of Europe that practice is starting. All over the world, wherever competition in telecommunications has been introduced, the consumer is getting a better deal. As the process of introducing more competition increases, that deal should get better and better.

Adding to the competition are the operators of the mobile telephone networks which have been immensely popular and whose prices are also falling. And waiting in the wings to get their services into operation sometime this side of 2000 are about half a dozen potential operators of satellite networks who plan to run a mobile phone service using low-orbit space-based satellites.

So the potential for price-cracking competition in communications services is with us, and the only question is how soon, how fast, prices will fall.

At the moment the main problem for the potential global nomad is that costs of sending video over the phone networks are high (though the cost of sending text is low). If governments around the world continue to drive deregulation and allow more and more competition, some quite dramatic changes in pricing could be seen before 2000.

If prices fall steeply, then the final plank in the platform providing the nomadic opportunity is in place. Adding together a cheap Nomadic Toolset, cheap communications links, cheap travel and the liberation of the ancient human urge to travel could unlock powerful forces.

The potential for nomadism has come about as the result of a series of liberations: liberation from the state monopolies that controlled telephone networks; liberation from the difficulty of operation and the prohibitive cost of computer power; liberation from the geographic ties of workplace and schooling; and political liberation from repressive regimes. Once repressed forces are liberated they can unleash extraordinary amounts of energy. The former Yugoslavia demonstrated tragically how liberation from repression can set free great energies which are then horribly misused.

A happier example of liberation is the computer industry itself. The advent of the PC liberated computing power from the control of 'men in white coats' in the 'computer room' and put it on many desks and in many homes. By doing that, enormous energies were released to devise and play video games, to design graphics, to surf the Internet and to send e-mail—among many other things.

So, when we are all liberated from the geographical ties of home and office, what energies will be released and how will we use them? What will happen if we can work anywhere? Will we prefer Pittsburgh to Phuket? Osaka to Bermuda? Liverpool to Provence? Frankfurt to Bali?

It's anyone's guess, but there's a fair chance that people will take the opportunity to move away from some of the uglier, more overcrowded places on our planet. And what will be the results of our new-found freedom to live where we want? What new stimuli will affect humans? Could we become a happier species?

One could easily envisage settlements growing around the world's more beautiful places where people could visit for a week or a month and then move on. With time-share apartments, holiday complexes like Club Med, and leisure villages, the concept is already established around the world. Whole towns could be built for temporary residents wandering from one ephemeral community to another.

If they were given the chance to establish nomadism as a mainstream human lifestyle for the first time for 10,000 years, what would people do with it? Could it, for instance, exaggerate differences between the sexes? Women have always been seen as more inclined to settle down than men—would cheap, available nomadism lead to even more disintegration of family life in the West than we are already experiencing? Or will it be the women who take off?

Given political and economic freedom to travel freely, people would have freedom to choose to which government they will pay their taxes. Governments might have to compete for citizens! Of course governments would all want the rich or high-earning ones, which could lead to some interesting countries. For instance, all the rich people would live in countries with low tax and few social services—and all the poor people would want to live in Scandinavia!

Almost certainly the dominant role of governments is set to diminish as national boundaries have less and less relevance to people and the pressures of global markets largely decide their policies for them.

As the influence of governments declines, and people's ties to a geographic region weaken, people will probably give their primary social allegiance to a group rather than to their country of origin. They might give it, for instance, to a company, to a sect, or to an interest group.

Who can tell? When social change meets new technological opportunities to release long-suppressed human instincts, the result could be the biggest revolution in human behaviour for 10,000 years—since humans relinquished the life of nomadic hunter-gatherers and settled down to farm.

Could ten millennia of settled existence turn out to have been a temporary aberration?

THE TRIGGER

'The cost of communications is going to zero
while the power of communications is
going to infinity.'
Herbert Henzler, Chairman, McKinsey Europe, 1996

W E are nomadic primitives. We try a bit of nomadism now and then but we don't have the support system to keep it up for long.

Nomadism can become a mainstream lifestyle only when three things change: attitudes, technology and communications.

All three are changing fast. In 1995 Japan held an exhibition of computers that could be worn. The computers were designed with parts that could be incorporated into clothing or which fitted conveniently to the body.

In 1995, British Telecom produced a prototype 'office-on-the-arm'—a strap-on computer with a visor which is operated by speech instead of a keyboard and can send faxes and e-mail, access the Internet and log into the office computer via the mobile phone network.

In April 1996, at an industry show in London, the US company Rockwell showed what it claimed to be the world's first commercially available wearable PC, called 'Trekker'. Trekker consists of a head unit, worn like a visor, and a PC attached to the belt weighing 3 pounds. It is powered by an ion lithium battery. Trekker's display is via an eyepiece for one eye attached to the visor. It is controlled by voice commands spoken into a microphone which is also attached to the visor.

Rockwell built Trekker to allow aerospace engineers to call up information or diagrams while keeping hands free and allowing total mobility. In 1996, Trekker cost £13,000, but Rockwell hopes to build smaller, cheaper versions. It gives the potential nomad the ability to carry easily enormous quantities of information.

Attitudes to carrying around technology have changed rapidly in the last decade, particularly among the young. Ten years ago the only piece of technology we routinely strapped on in the morning was a wristwatch.

Now there are few executives who don't put their mobile phone into their briefcase before leaving for work. Many will also carry a laptop computer or will slip a palmtop computer into a handbag or a coat pocket.

Nomadic communication: Whenever, Wherever, With anybody, By any media

The Age of Nomadism

Companies nowadays see no reason why their executives should not always be contactable. Similarly, companies see no reason why executives should not work during those hours spent on planes, waiting at airports or holed up in hotels.

Like it or not, it is difficult to buck the corporate trend. If you want to be upwardly mobile professionally, you need to be a mobile professional.

Outside the workplace, the usefulness of the nomadic tools currently available is not yet so compelling that most of us willingly carry them around.

The electronics industry is betting on a change. It senses that, with homes chock-full of electronic products, the next consumer boom will be for personal products—products that are wearable, pocketable or carryable.

Imagination is currently running ahead of capability. The industry can see the prize but can't grasp it. There is always a limitation—either of technology or in the communications networks—which puts the prize tantalisingly out of reach.

Look at the 'personal digital assistant' produced by Apple Computer and called 'Newton'. The hype suggested that it was a pocketable computer which could communicate anywhere. The reality was that you had to plug it into a telephone jack socket to do any communicating.

Imagine trying to sell a mobile phone that you had to plug into a telephone jack! The original Newton failed to meet sales expectations, as did a similar product called 'EO' made by the American telecommunications giant AT&T.

EO could be put in your pocket, you could write messages on it with a pen, the messages would be converted into a digital file and sent anywhere on the phone network. It sounds good, but EO was a disappointment because, like Newton, it had to be plugged into the wall.

Plugging things into wall sockets is always a problem if you're travelling. If you are away from home and office, finding a telephone jack socket can be a lot of hassle.

Many telephones are still 'hard-wired', i.e. do not have a plug which can be connected and disconnected, but instead are wired directly from the body of the telephone into the wall socket.

The really committed, technically attuned nomad may, at that stage, decide to unscrew the socket on the wall and dismantle the plug on the computer and then try to match up the wires in the socket to the wires in the plug—which could be as many as eight. It can take hours.

Even assuming that you do find a telephone with a jack socket—and someone prepared to let you use it—many people simply don't like having to ask a favour.

If you are abroad, the problems mount up alarmingly. Trying to get connected to the telephone network using a laptop computer and a modem can be a nightmare. For instance, actually plugging a computer or a modem into a phone line in a foreign country can be a major problem. Plugs and sockets differ around the world.

And even if today's primitive nomad has the right plug to fit the foreign socket, there's the problem of the dialling tone. Dialling tones vary around the world. The dialling tone sent down the phone line by the nomad's modem may not be recognised by a foreign telephone exchange.

So it is not only a problem getting a physical connection via plug and socket into a foreign phone network, it is also a problem making an electronic connection by getting the foreign phone line to recognise the dialling tone of your tools.

And that's all before you start dealing with the hassles and delays of logging onto the Internet and trying to find out whatever it is you want—a process described as using the telephone system without a telephone directory.

Of course, for the mobile executive who has to travel as part of the job, it is worth carrying around all the paraphernalia of assorted plugs, sockets and diallers. But it's a lot of kit. Given a choice, many of us wouldn't bother to pack it.

There's a simple answer—use radio links to get into the phone network. Using radio links you can be sitting in a bar or a car, in an office reception or an airport waiting lounge, and you can send information to and from a laptop as easily as using a mobile phone.

This is the capability which the electronics industry thinks everyone will want—the 'killer app' (application).

The industry's ideal product will be both more and less than a laptop computer. It will do more communicating and less computing. And it will be much smaller and lighter than today's laptops.

It will be a tool which you can put in your pocket and take down to the beach. On the beach you can take a photo with a digital camera, transfer the photo as a digital file into the tool, then send it, via radio links, as an e-mail over the Internet to granny.

For a lot of money, and using fixed phone lines rather than radio links, that can be done today. There was consternation at the spring 1996 fashion shows caused by digital cameras. Photographs of the Parisian couturiers' latest creations were being taken by digital cameras, transferred to Macintosh laptop computers, then squirted down the phone lines to the Far East where work on 'cloning' the new clothes could be instantly started.

Those cameras in Paris cost $14,000 and the Macintoshes had to use telephone lines, not radio. But before the end of the same year—in the autumn of 1996—digital cameras were on the market for under $500—not with such high definition as the ones seen at the spring fashion shows, but good enough for the family photo album. That's a measure of how fast the electronics industry can move down the price/performance curve with a hot new technology.

We can be sure that the industry will be delivering the same capability over wireless radio links, in a pocketable form, for a consumer price within a few years.

Back on our early 21st century beach, as well as spraying the ether with photos to granny, we'll be using this tool to access our travel agent's computer to check or change travel arrangements.

Workaholics will use it to send or pick up messages from the office computer and to videoconference. Net-aholics will use it to access a World Wide Web site or browse the Internet. All from a deckchair using radio links.

You could do some of that today. Already it's quite possible to buy a portable worldwide communicating system based on satellites. It will send messages—voice, fax and e-mail—from anywhere in the world to anywhere else. But it needs a big suitcase weighing over 15 pounds to fit it all in, and it costs about the same as a small car.

That will look laughable in a few years' time. It will be like showing modern teenagers, familiar with credit-card sized radios, a 1950s-vintage 'wireless set'—walnut-encased, valve-based and mains-driven.

From the 'wireless set' to the credit-card radio took 40 years of technological evolution. But to go from the 15-pound communicating suitcase to the pocket communicator will take only a few years, because the pace of change is accelerating.

For instance, the first portable telephones required 12-pound battery packs to be lugged around with them; modern mobiles fit in a shirt pocket and weigh little.

Mobiles in 1996 are so small and light they are already starting to take on other communications functions without losing their portability. For instance, a good many phones in Europe built for Europe's GSM (Groupe Spéciale Mobile) digital wireless network also link into laptop computers. By connecting mobile phone and computer you can send a fax or an e-mail using radio links to get access to the phone system.

Digital wireless networks are going to be a key facilitator for nomadism. Europe's GSM is the world's first digital wireless network. Japan's digital wireless network, PHS (Personal Handiphone System), started operations in 1995.

In America digital wireless networks only started to get under way in 1996, propelled by the sheer weight of money paid by potential operators to get licences to operate from the government.

In 1995, the big US telecommunications companies—mostly AT&T and Sprint—paid $7.7 billion for licences to operate digital wireless networks. Then, in February 1996, President Clinton signed the Telecommunications Act 1996 which allowed more competition and, in the subsequent three weeks, over $9 billion was raised in auctions of licences. With some $17 billion already committed, companies are keen to get their networks up and running to start recouping the licence fees. All eyes are on 1997 for large-scale operations.

When Europe, Japan and the USA all have digital wireless networks in place, one key factor for nomadism is in place. There remains the other one—the tools.

The mobile phone/laptop combination may give access to the Internet or to the office computer without having to worry about wires or different socket types, but it is far from ideal.

Apart from the vagaries of all mobile phone networks—dead periods, cut-offs, etc.—there is still the problem of the amount of kit you have to carry around to send messages over the mobile phone network.

For instance you need to carry the mobile phone, the phone's battery charger, the laptop computer, the laptop's power supply, and different regional plugs for the electricity supply for the phone recharger and the laptop. That amount of kit represents a lot of hassle and weight and is an unattractive proposition for anyone to carry around except for work.

The great moment for the nomadic age will be when one tool can handle wireless communications of all kinds—voice, documents, text, fax, video, broadcast TV, still pictures. When such a tool is as ubiquitous and as robust as the fax machine, nomadism can take off. It will come—but few people are prepared to predict the exact year. Five years is possible, but it could take ten.

In the interim, the electronics industry will come out with a string of products which will edge ever closer to this ideal. In 1996 we saw the first combinations of a mobile phone with palmtop computer all in one pocketable package.

In April 1996 Hewlett-Packard announced a combination of a Nokia GSM mobile telephone and a palmtop computer called 'OmniGo 700LX'. The unit looks like a mobile phone, then opens along the long side to reveal keyboard and screen.

Nokia also came up in 1996 with a product called 'Communicator 9000' for the GSM network which provides a similar combination of computer and mobile phone in a package weighing one pound. Users could send and receive faxes 'wirelessly' through the mobile phone network and tap into other computers. The Communicator 9000 contains Internet browser software and e-mail services. It is possible to read an e-mail on it while making a phone call. It can send data to and from PCs and printers via a cable or an infra-red link. It sold for around $1,000 in 1996 and sold 100,000 units in the first six months of being marketed. The enthusiasm with which it was taken up demonstrated a user demand for the concept which other manufacturers are anxious to follow.

These first combinations of mobile phone and computer look just like that—a phone tagged onto a computer. More elegant products should be on the way, but there are problems with putting a computer and a mobile telephone in one unit. The main problem is the interference between the circuitry which does the computing and the circuitry which does the communicating.

Some companies, for instance Motorola, say they have solved the interference problem. If they have, others will. So we can expect to see more elegant, streamlined examples of communicating computers. That's because it has been the chief concern of the electronics industry, these last 40 years, to shrink its products into smaller boxes. The great example is the computer which has gone from a roomful to a lap-full in that period.

Look in the High Street shop windows and you increasingly see electronic goods which are amalgamations of different products. For instance, at the Telecom 95 industry show in Geneva, Canon's 'Hyper Media Platform' combined a colour desktop video-conferencing unit, a colour printer, a scanner, a plain paper fax machine, a telephone, a copier, and a video camera. Similarly, Olivetti's 'Envision' went on sale in late 1995 which put together a PC, a compact disc player, a hi-fi, a fax and an answerphone in a single machine.

Combined PC/TVs are common, combination fax/phone/ answerphone machines are routine, laptop computers usually have slots into which you can put modems, and it is becoming possible to buy slot-in cards containing the functions of wireless telephones.

Fax machines are merging with printers, and mobile phones are taking on computing functions like word processing and the sending and receiving of faxes.

Meanwhile, desktop computers are combining every type of electronic product: modem, phone, videophone, mobile phone, camcorder, camera, fax, calculator, organiser, etc., as well as TV.

With every electronic product taking on more and more of the functions of other electronic products, you might wonder whether the Complete Nomadic Toolset will be a mobile phone with computing functions? Or a computer with mobile telephone functions. Or an organiser with a mobile phone incorporated in it? Or even a hand-held games machine with some computer/organiser/telephone features?

The answer is it will be all of them. Companies today making each of these equipment types are looking to add the functions of other equipment types to their products.

But pity the industry's executives who may have grown up in a company specialising in one equipment type and find they now have to wrap their brains around entirely new industrial sectors.

For an executive in the staid telecommunications industry it is a major culture shift to understand the wackier games machine industry; and from the conformity of the PC industry—where all the products from the different companies are essentially the same—it is a long step to the organiser industry where products differ considerably.

No industry executive can hope to know exactly what mix of functions of computer, mobile phone, organiser and games

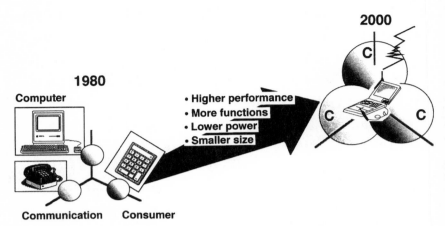

Market Convergence in the Nomadic Age

machine the consumer will go for. And the consumer, not having been offered these choices before, doesn't know either.

Manufacturers become schizophrenic—not certain, any more, what business they are in. Mobile phone manufacturers worry about whether they are becoming computer manufacturers when they add computing functions to mobile phones, and computer manufacturers worry that they're getting into the telecommunications business.

That's why the mid-90s is a difficult time for the world's technology companies. As all the different products merge into each other, they are having to get into areas which they thought were the province of other companies.

This causes executives terrible anxieties. Small wonder that the 90s have seen a rash of companies from different disciplines getting together in consortia and joint ventures. These consortia have become such a common feature of the high-tech business that the Chairman of Intel, Dr Gordon Moore, has scornfully dubbed them 'group gropes'.

The best-known consortium is General Magic. This includes some of the world's biggest high-tech hitters: AT&T, NTT of Japan, France Télécom and Sony. It looks at future product concepts and the technologies they will require.

There are a host of collaborations between the manufacturers of PCs, mobile phones, games machines and 'Internet Computers'—stripped-down computers linking the TV to the phone line to provide Internet access. If you want to make 'Internet Computers' you need the help of almost everyone because it takes in elements of the games machine, the mobile phone and the PC.

Furthermore, the Internet Computer is a brand new product concept, first described in 1995 by Larry Ellison, Chairman of Oracle, with the first examples appearing in 1996.

So for the industry, the phenomenon of the merging of equipment types is a major headache. But for the user, merging equipment types is a plus because the more they merge into a single unit, the less you have to bother with multiple plugs, multiple power supplies, wires and connectors.

The industry trend has been that computers have shrunk in size by an order of magnitude every ten years. So a computer which typically occupied 100,000 cubic centimetres of space in 1970 had become reduced in size to 10,000 cubic centimetres by 1980 and to 1,000 by 1990, and will be down to 100 cubic centimetres by 2000.

The pace of this shrinking has been predictable for the past 35 years, as explained in Chapter 4. Therefore it's possible to say when all the equipment types needed in the Complete Nomadic Toolset can be combined in a portable, pocketable form.

The optimum form may well be the organiser. Organisers are specifically built to fit into a jacket or trouser pocket. They are light enough to carry around permanently without being a nuisance. Typically they allow a bit of word processing, a big store of addresses and phone numbers and sometimes some spreadsheet functions. With an external modem they can send data down phone wires and can send faxes. They also act as calculators, diaries, alarm clocks, reminder calendars (beeping to get attention), and world time guides. They are usually inexpensive—less than $300.

To these functions, the organiser manufacturers want to add wireless communications, both voice and data. The leading organiser manufacturer, Psion of the UK, began the most expensive project in its history in 1995—recruiting a team of telecommunications specialists to add radio links to its organisers. By adding radio links to an organiser, an organiser becomes a combined mobile phone, fax, answering machine and computer.

Furthermore, the organiser makers want to add voice recognition capabilities so that you can record a message, store it like a text file or send it down a phone line to another computer which can either print it, display it, or speak it.

Other abilities being added to the organiser are infra-red communications (as in TV remote controls) which, over short distances, allow organisers to exchange information with a PC.

Indeed, two organisers each with infra-red connections can 'sense' each other and start transferring information without human intervention—which conjures up a slightly alarming prospect of machines chatting away to each other without being told to.

Something else which is being incorporated into organisers is the ability to 'scan' words and store them in its memory. Scanning means you pass an optical character reader in the organiser over a document and the machine recognises the words and converts them into a digital file. Once in the form of a digital file the words can be transferred over telephone wires or over mobile phone links or stored on a magnetic disc, a chip or a CD-ROM.

Another feature manufacturers are refining is 'handwriting re-cognition': you write with a pen on the organiser's screen and the organiser recognises the words and stores them as a text file.

Of course, not only the organiser manufacturers are pursuing all these capabilities. The mobile phone manufacturers, the palmtop computer manufacturers, the games machines manufacturers—all of them are looking at adding these functions to their products.

So the Complete Nomadic Toolset may well not come from the organiser manufacturers—it could equally well come from the phone, computer or games makers. It is an industry Holy Grail.

Even when we have it, however, the Complete Nomadic Toolset does not, by itself, allow us to be nomads. The tool is only as useful as the information it can pick up.

Marooned on a desert island, still running your business or doing your job, wanting to stay in touch with friends and family, looking forward to new films and videos, needing to pick up the TV programmes and latest newscasts, you'll need more than just a tool, you'll need a communications infrastructure.

In a primitive form you can see this structure emerging now with today's Internet. Awkward to access, difficult to find your way around and expensive to use, today's Internet could become a user-friendly, accessible, inexpensive and universal information/ education/entertainment network.

In the 'Cyberia' chain of cafés in London, Edinburgh, Manchester, Kingston-upon-Thames and Tokyo people are being introduced to the Internet by paying for time on a PC connected to the Internet and, with help if required, are shown how to 'surf'— flitting through what's on offer and experiencing what they fancy.

Cyberia reckon they've introduced over 100,000 people to the Internet. At the moment, to use the Internet, you need a computer, a modem, and the software link to the net. The modem plugs the computer into the telephone wires and the software connects you to the net; it seems a simple process that allows your computer to talk to any other computer. But, but, but . . .

Many people find it a difficult process. It can take time to 'log on'—the phrase meaning to get a telephone connection set up between the computer and the Internet access point. Once a connection is established, people find it very difficult to find what they want, or indeed to find anything they want.

It can be expensive because it takes time to find what you want, and time on the line is still expensive these days; and as a communications tool it can be frustrating because the time it takes for messages to arrive at their destinations can vary wildly, from ten minutes to ten hours.

The reason for the unpredictable time involved in message sending and receiving is the structure of the Internet itself as a network of millions of computers. When a message is sent from, say, Paris to London, it may be routed via Boston where it could sit on a computer for hours waiting to be picked up and sent on to the next computer in the link.

It is unpredictable when a 'message box' on an Internet computer is going to be accessed and its contents re-routed to the next link in the chain. Projects are afoot to find ways to speed up messaging.

On the other hand this random structure of interlinked computers provides one of the beauties of the Internet. Being an organic structure, with new people and organisations constantly linking up to it, the development of the Internet is driven by the 'democratic' demands and ideas of millions of users rather than by an overseeing bureaucracy.

That democratic future is, in the absence of government interference, assured because anyone able to spend $5+ a month can connect up to it and anyone can put information or entertainment onto it. And anyone can make products which make it easier to use.

In that respect, the Internet is a democratic structure—and interesting because its development potential is both unpredictable and limitless.

But although the Internet's structure is in place and its potential as a global information exchange/market is assured, at the moment it is still a primitive form of communication and is used by most people for fairly mundane purposes.

People 'log on' to 'talk' to people in interest groups, to access electronic libraries carried on computers in foreign universities, to call up databases to check facts, to call up pictures from art galleries.

People also call up so-called 'Web pages' on 'Web sites' which various organisations pay to put on the Internet to provide details of their products, or examples of their services to attract customers or give information to existing customers.

According to the Internet Business Centre's own statistics, there were 100,000 Web sites on the Internet at the end of August 1995 but nearly 246,000 by the end of November 1995, showing very rapid growth. By April 1996 the number has been estimated in the millions.

The same source claimed that, in November 1995, there were 47 million people in the world with Internet access. Estimates for April 1996 more than double this number. This seems a staggering statistic.

More realistically, if you look at the number of subscribers—people or organisations paying their $5 or more a month to companies which provide a connection to the Internet—this is less than a tenth of the 47 million claimed to have Internet access.

There is certainly a massive rush of interest among businesses of all kinds. Newspapers and magazines put selections of their output on the Internet; banks and building societies put information on their pages from which you can get quotes for loans and mortgages; World Inc. of San Francisco has put a programme called 'Worlds Chat' on the Internet that you can download onto your computer and that allows you to take on a 'cyberform' such as a fish or a teddy bear and move around a 3-D 'cyber world' chatting to other cyberforms representing real people!

So far, general businesses, as opposed to specialist providers of Internet-related products, have not yet tapped the potential gold in the hills of the Internet. Companies are generally aware of the Internet but for them it is difficult to find a way of making it pay.

One sort of Web site that can pay is used to show a series of services on offer and then to charge for electing to go for a higher level of services. It's possible to charge for each higher level. The problem for the service provider remains getting the money. Credit cards are the obvious way but once put on the Internet, your credit card details are, potentially, known to 47 million people.

So ways of making payment are being explored. Also ways of checking financial references of organisations with which you want to do business are being developed. Clearly most business-men would feel a little uneasy about doing business with a 'cyber-customer'.

However, there's one class of companies which have found the Internet a goldmine. They are the access providers with their small but steady subscriptions from individual users coming in every month.

They can grow into significant sized companies fast. For in-stance, the UK service provider Demon Internet was valued by the London Stock Exchange at £26.5 million after only three years in existence, by which time it had signed up 50,000 subscribers pay-ing £10 a month.

Those people who set up Web sites for companies and organ-isations have also made a killing during 1994–97. That's because company managements have felt increasingly uneasy about being left out of something that could be a major revenue earner. So those consultants who specialise in setting up Web sites have done well in the mid-90s.

However, according to a 1996 survey by KPMG Peat Marwick, few managers were able to justify their participation on economic grounds.

Advertising on the Internet—usually included on the Web sites of information providers like newspapers or magazines—is estimated to be a $172m business in 1996, according to Forrester Research. In fact such content providers have only been able to make money from their Web sites by attracting such advertisements. Forrester estimates that advertisement revenue from the Internet will be $2.57bn by the year 2000.

It is not thought that content providers will be able to charge significantly for access to their Web sites. For instance Forrester estimates that in 2000 the total amount of subscriptions to Web sites—$206m—will be worth less than a tenth of the total advertising revenue.

Another group of companies which have found gold on the Internet are those who provide the all important software which makes the Internet useful by allowing users to scour the net for what they want.

This kind of software is called a 'browser'. In effect it is like an index in a book. If you want to find something in a book, you look it up in the index to find the relevant page. Similarly, on the Internet, if you want to find something you type in a reference and the browser will locate a computer on which the information you want is stored.

One browser company, Netscape, was valued at $2 billion on the US stock market in June 1995 when it was only about 14 months old. Its only product, called the 'Navigator', quickly became the world's most popular browser.

Expected to form a big future market are what are called 'intelligent agents', sometimes known as 'software robots'. Like worker spiders these agents crawl all over the net carrying out pre-programmed tasks.

In 1996, France Télécom is running a trial of intelligent agents called 'Pyramid'. The technology has been licensed from the US consortium General Magic.

BT is developing a service based on intelligent agents that will locate people and deliver messages to them in the most appropriate form for the circumstances, e.g. converting voice to fax, or an e-mail to a telephone.

It is generally thought that intelligent agents will become a key facilitator for making the Internet useful to users. They will wade through the mountains of irrelevant data on the net to provide precisely what has been asked for in a user's brief. For instance, they could search for a list of sources of all the parts needed to build a car, or search for all the newspaper articles on a particular subject, or find out the best price available on a particular product.

Intelligent agents could undertake much of the work of people in the distribution business. Having identified someone's needs the agents could simply instruct Federal Express to deliver the goods and arrange for payment.

Another opportunity to make money on the Internet is expected to be the provision of 'interactive' services—buying and selling on the Internet.

Using an Internet interactive service, a start-up company anywhere in the world can access the entire world market by putting its services or products on the Internet. That's a mind-boggling prospect for companies in the Third World which would normally have little chance of reaching foreign markets until they could afford to send salesmen abroad, or appoint foreign distributors.

Attractive it may be in theory, but there are two major snags to doing business over the Internet. As already mentioned, one is the security problem. Secure ways of 'encrypting' or encoding payments for goods and services over the Internet are currently being devised but are not yet a reality.

However, a number of proposed methods of paying over the Internet are at advanced stages of development. For instance, the Mondex 'electronic purse' concept, which has been trialled in Swindon in the UK since mid-1995 and is backed by the NatWest and Midland banks, provides a means by which cash can be loaded onto a 'smartcard' (a chip-based debit card) and which can make electronic cash transfers from and to a bank or between cardholders.

Another proposed method for making payments over the Internet has come from IBM and Europay, the latter backed by Mastercard and Visa, who have suggested a payment method called Inter-Keyed Payment (iKP) protocol that can work with PC operating systems such as Windows and Macintosh.

A third method of payment has been devised by Visa and Microsoft but it needs a proprietary system to work rather than standard PCs and operating systems.

In order to make the various systems work, it will be necessary to have card readers that can be fitted onto a PC or TV. These readers are being developed for the market.

Also mobile phone manufacturers are thinking of including a Mondex slot which will allow people to make electronic transfers over the Internet using their mobile phones.

So the development of methods for making payment over the net are well advanced and should be a practicable proposition in the late 1990s, so long as the security problems can be cracked.

Security is needed not just for payments; it's needed for contract exchange, product details and delivery arrangements, not to mention copyrights, patents and trade-secret kinds of intellectual property. Doing deals in public is not the current commercial practice of many companies.

The second major snag to doing business over the Internet is the time it takes for messages to arrive. It can be extremely frustrating to try and settle a transaction when the time for getting a reply to a proposal can take from ten minutes to ten hours.

Both problems are being worked on. Software which routes messages much more efficiently through the maze of computers is being developed, and enormous amounts of brainpower are being expended to create security on the Internet. It can safely be assumed that these efforts will succeed in the next five years, and maybe much sooner.

That's not to say that the amount of business being done on the Internet today is trivial. According to Forrester Research, even by 1994 it was already worth $240 million. According to Peter Cunningham, founder of the international research company Input, by the year 2000 trade on the Internet 'will potentially exceed $200 billion'. However, Forrester Research's projection for trade on the Internet in the year 2000 is $6.9 billion, while the projection of another research group, Simba Information, is $24 billion for worldwide sales on the net by 1999. Those estimates are in startling contrast to Cunningham's figure and indicate that there's an element of guesswork in these projections.

Internet-based trading exchanges are the dream of many people who see big potential returns for establishing 'electronic trading floors' on the Internet. The idea is to trade commodities like shares, coffee beans or metals futures on a worldwide basis.

However, so far the Internet is probably not quite up to this sort of usage, though private subscriber systems such as the Mitsubishi-Electric-backed UK company Infotrade have set up a telephone-based share trading system using proprietary access and software for subscribers only. From there it is but a short step to trading on the Internet.

As the Internet cracks its technical problems, these sort of electronic trading floors could become available to everyone, resulting in a vast increase in global trade and huge profits for the middlemen taking commissions on the deals. It is an idea whose time will come.

For the nomad, of course, the Internet promises everything, though it may deliver little now. Eventually you can see the nomad using the Internet to dial up a song, or a video, or a picture, or a computer program, or a map showing him where he is, or to tune into remote TV cameras to see other parts of the world.

As the links go digital, more and more information types will be transferred. Already we're seeing photographs taken by digital cameras being squirted down telephone wires to be displayed on PC screens. And already it is getting to be reasonably inexpensive (say $300) to buy a 'Voice Organiser' which can record a spoken message, convert it into a digital file and store or transfer it like any other file. So long as the receiving PC has a speaker, it can speak out such a message. Where both PCs have speakers, an Internet connection and voice recognition, the PC users can send each other spoken messages just as on a telephone.

The beauty of this for users is that they can send their message to the ends of the Earth for the price of a local phone call. The nightmare for telephone network operators like BT or AT&T is that it could put them out of business. At present, of course, that wouldn't happen because Internet messages tend to take a long time to arrive. However, software is being commercialised that can speed this up.

IBM has developed software which makes phone calls over the Internet possible for the price of local calls. It is adding this to its PCs as an extra feature in 1996. IBM also hopes to be using the same techniques to add videoconferencing to its PCs by 1998.

So the prospect looms of people using the Internet to speak to each other just as they do on the telephone. This prospect is giving the telephone network operators a headache or two. Not only will their long-distance business collapse, but they will find it difficult to charge at all because the time on the line for a digitised message is so short compared to that for a spoken message.

The next step will be sending camcorder pictures from wherever you are to wherever you like. This will require a considerable increase in the carrying capability ('bandwidth') of the communications networks. Imminent, dramatic increases in carrying capability are described in Chapter 6. When combined with the emergence of the Complete Nomadic Toolset, these form the trigger for 21st century nomadism. It will soon be pulled.

THE NOMADIC URGE

'Travel is the world's largest industry in terms of
gross output, approaching $3.4trn. It employs 204m
people worldwide, or one in every nine workers—
10.6% of the global workforce.'
John Naisbitt, Global Paradox, *1994*

T HE European president of one of the world's top technology companies does not have an office. His working week is spent travelling round the company's European operations which report to him.

It is less costly for the company if the boss goes to visit the operations which he controls, than if teams of people from those operations disrupt their work by having to constantly fly to see the boss.

The president of this company has a secretary in Europe who keeps his diary and who can tell callers where the boss is and a number at which he can be contacted at any time.

While on the move, he keeps in touch via a mobile phone. When he's in an office or in a hotel room he can plug his portable computer into the phone jack and download and reply to his e-mail.

When in the air, he can use the airline's phones and expects, soon, to be travelling with a number of airlines currently planning to offer a phone jack facility for laptops. When that happens he will hardly ever be out of touch with any of the offices he supervises.

His wife hardly ever sees this man. He is a new breed of person for whom the world's high-tech companies are increasingly geared up to cater—the Mobile Professional.

More and more mobile professionals are being spawned every year. While some of these—the top ones—travel to supervise the operations under their own control, most mobile professionals are travelling to meet customers and potential customers.

As companies try to operate in more and more countries, with many more companies nowadays aspiring to operate globally, they put ever-increasing pressure on their executives to travel.

Globalised accountants' firms send accountants across the world to audit customers' books; investment bankers roam the world advising on the feasibility of projects and raising capital; stockbrokers travel the world seeking stock buyers; every kind of salesman is on the move.

As companies manage global businesses, many of their managers spend hours on aeroplanes flying to and from meetings. As products and services become more sophisticated those who sell and support them have increasingly specialised skills, and wherever knowledge and skills are in short supply, employers will maximise them by using them as widely as possible.

All these trends lead to ever-increasing numbers of these global business itinerants. As companies require them to travel more, so the tools of communication are becoming more advanced and more portable. There is less need for the mobile professional to spend time at a fixed office.

Companies could be heading more towards the model of a wandering tribe than a fixed entity with fixed offices and staff. Take the business phenomenon of 'hot-desking'. This developed when companies started to appreciate that their more skilled employees were working to individual schedules rather than to common patterns. Quite clearly if they were not working to similar routines, they did not need to meet every day at the same time in the same place.

Companies then started to realise that a good deal of their expensive office space was not being used. One British facilities management consultancy, Procord, has estimated that, even during the working day, about 40% of all office space is unused. Since working days represent only a third of total available time, this means that on average any particular piece of office space is being used for only about 13% of the 24 hours.

One of the basic credos of management is constantly to review costs and to cut them where they are unjustifiable. The costs of leasing office space are high, and if the space is not being used then it is clearly a cost that should be cut. But how? To many companies, the answer is to recognise that there is no further need to keep to the traditional office structure of one desk per person.

If employees are going to be away from their usual place of work for half their working days, it is logical to save on space by letting two people share a desk. That is the practice at the London offices of international accountants Ernst & Young where there are half as many desks as staff.

If employees are in the office for only a quarter of their working time, it makes sense to have four people to a desk. Four to a desk is the ratio which IBM UK expects to achieve by the year 2000. At the San Francisco headquarters of the international consultancy company Andersen Consulting, the number is already five per desk. Thus instead of having personalised workspaces, every workspace has to be usable by everyone and every space will have a networked computer which anyone can use. Once that is achieved, any company employee can work equally well at any company office.

Clearly companies are all in favour of hot-desking because it saves on office space costs. It also saves on secretarial staff. For instance, the American computer company DEC runs a so-called 'telecentre' at Basingstoke in the UK where 80 'hot-desks' are staffed by eight secretaries.

The next cost-saving step—already being worked on—is to develop unstaffed offices where employees can just drop in to use the computers and communications systems to download or upload information and communicate with colleagues before moving on.

So flexible is the possibility of this kind of office that it could be made portable. When the company feels it needs an office some-where it can rent space, or maybe just a hotel room, wheel in the equipment, plug it in, and a 'virtual office' is created for as long as it is needed.

Purpose-built 'business centres' are already a familiar sight in airports, hotels and even shopping complexes. One of the world's top business centre operators, the UK company Regus, recognises that customers are now looking for more and more sophisticated equipment which allows them to work from a business centre as easily as they would from a company office.

Increasingly customers are wanting videoconferencing links and Regus has some 50 business centres with videoconferencing facil-ities in Europe using both proprietary products such as PictureTel's dedicated videoconferencing systems as well as the kind of plug-in videoconferencing board that can be attached to a PC.

As technologically advanced office suites with the latest com-puters and videoconferencing links become generally available, it is possible that companies might find them a cost-effective alter-native to taking out a multi-year lease on an office building.

If a meeting is required between employees who have no office to go to, they can each hire office suites with videoconferencing facil-ities and set up a meeting. Not one of them need be in a company office and the videoconferencing links can be global if need be.

Already most sizeable companies use hotels liberally for man-agement meetings and presentations. They find that the traditional office environment has too many interruptions and distractions and may not be secure.

These trends are giving facilities managers a good many headaches figuring out what exactly the role of an office will be in the 21st century, if indeed it will have any role.

'Teleworking' or working from home has been a much-touted way of work for 20 years without becoming mainstream. But, as more jobs are related to the provision of information, it becomes more possible for work to be farmed out to home-workers.

A good many American companies are finding that it is cost-effective to get routine information processing—for instance, managing electronic archives or files—done in places such as India where labour costs are lower, the language is English and there are plenty of educated people to do the work. Fitted up with a computer, a modem and a telephone line, a resident of Delhi can process information as effectively as if they were occupying high-cost space in a company's New York office, and at a fraction of a New York salary.

Financial calculations which make managements weigh up the viability of Third World teleworkers against local staff, or balance the economics of multi-year leases on offices against hiring offices in business centres, could make the traditional idea of the office redundant.

Within some offices the change of thinking is already apparent. Instead of rows of desks where workers process information in solitude, modern companies have informal meeting spaces and presentation rooms, more like hotels than traditional offices—places where ideas and reports are exchanged.

These changes reflect the emergence of the business nomad. The nomadic company employee is well on the way to becoming a mainstream lifestyle even without the development of an affordable, pocketable, ubiquitous Complete Nomadic Toolset. When that tool does becomes available, with all its supporting infrastructure, then nomadic employees may outnumber those who commute on a daily basis to the same place of work. Nomad vs Commuter could be one of the most significant lifestyle choices of the 21st century.

Just as the employee can become of no fixed abode, so can the company. The decline of the importance of 'Head Office' is having a major impact on the concept of the company itself.

Nowadays we think of companies as having an address and a nationality—even as being wedded to a particular city. We think of IBM as an American company headquartered in Armonk; of Matsushita as a Japanese company headquartered in Osaka; of Siemens as a German company from Munich. However, reality is already becoming blurred as such companies operate globally, employ citizens of many different states, pay taxes to many different countries and can choose any region of the world to establish their operations.

Nowadays companies find China an excellent location for low-cost manufacturing; they find India a fertile place to run a software operation; they find Russia rich in mathematical skills; they find California supreme for innovating in microelectronics. A company can design a product in Detroit, manufacture it in Shanghai, write the software in Bombay, develop the microelectronics in San Jose and devise the algorithms for it in Moscow.

As companies scatter their manufacturing, R&D, design and marketing operations around the world, so they can site their headquarters wherever they want in the world.

At the moment, companies are constrained from moving away from their traditional 'home' base by loyalty, the lure of government protection and procurement and, in some cases, the wish of their top people (and the top people's partners) to be in familiar environments.

But that is changing. The effect of local government procurement and protected local markets is bound to diminish as global trading conditions are gradually enforced throughout the world. Some of the more enlightened companies already recognise that; for instance NEC of Japan has set itself the target of having 50% of its sales coming from goods manufactured outside Japan by the end of the decade.

Companies, particularly high-tech companies, realise that they have to be worldwide traders, and it is the aim of trade regulatory bodies like the World Trade Organisation working with agreements like GATT to encourage common working, trading and market conditions among its membership.

As far as the preferences of top executives and their partners are concerned, executive nomadism means that more and more of them are becoming familiar with foreign lifestyles—and in many cases enjoying them.

When local advantage and local prejudice are diminished, where will a company locate itself? When the location of its headquarters will make no difference to the efficient running of the company, where will it go? The answer could very well be where it gets the best deal.

If the headquarters is just an office building, that is probably going to become less important as the nerve-centre of a business as operations are global and nomadic executives meet in video-conferences. However, a building is easily vacated. If it is the legally registered office of the company, this is also readily switched. For years we've seen companies which own oil tankers registering them in Liberia to get an especially relaxed regulatory regime, and throughout the 1990s we've seen companies changing nationality to take their headquarters out of Hong Kong prior to the handover to China.

If the headquarters is the company's corporate 'memory'—its files, personnel and payroll records, archives, proprietary technologies, operational records, etc.—these are also highly mobile because they are kept on a computer. With the push of a button the entire contents of the corporate database can be transferred to another computer. It doesn't matter where that computer is, or whether the company owns it or not—it might be that there are particularly good rental terms for hiring space on a computer in Ulan Bator—the corporate 'HQ' could be transferred to it in seconds.

So, as well as the company's employees being nomadic, the company itself could become nomadic. Its staff would be something akin to a wandering tribe. Like the pastoral nomads of ancient times it would look for a pasture, settle—then move on. The advantage of being nomadic would be that it bestows power.

Not only would a nomadic company be free to scout around for the best deals by which to rent computer space for the corporate database, it could also seek out the most favourable regulatory regime, the lowest tax rates, the most obliging financiers, the most willing workforces.

If companies ever decided to exercise the power over governments which nomadism would give them, they would be able to extract increasingly attractive deals from governments wanting to be host country for their headquarters—and presumably the bulk of their tax liability.

How far governments might go in trying to attract companies to set up in their countries can be seen from the lengths to which they go today to persuade companies to locate factories and research centres within their borders. Companies are routinely offered large incentive packages by regional development bodies—which are underwritten by governments—sometimes amounting to 20% or more of the total investment costs of a project.

Particularly attractive to governments are manufacturing operations which employ large numbers of people. Among the incentives which governments queue up to offer companies are free land, free factory buildings, low-interest or even interest-free loans, grants, free training, free electricity, free water, tax holidays and, very often, the promise of a suitably prestigious figure from politics or, if there's a monarchy, from the royal family, to open the factory.

In 1995, the Prime Minister of the UK, John Major, personally lobbied the president of Siemens, Heinrich von Pierer, to get him to locate a factory in the north of England rather than in Austria.

The level of urgency with which government agencies now pursue the multinationals—particularly in the high-tech industries—shows how far they feel that future employment prospects lie in their hands.

In the electronics area, some governments like those of Canada, the Republic of Ireland and, increasingly, the UK have set themselves up principally as a base for subsidiaries of foreign multinationals without a matching regard for trying to develop a significant indigenously owned industry.

Politicians in such countries are fond of saying that the ownership of industry is not important; what is important is the investment and the jobs it creates. From their point of view it means more people paying taxes and it makes the export figures look better.

But it might be wondered how much of a hostage to fortune politicians are presenting to their successors who might face the dilemma of choosing between the interests of foreign companies and the interests of their own citizens.

As countries embrace international norms such as democratic capitalism, the international monetary system and the GATT trading structure, they obviously restrict their governments' freedom of action.

Governments which, in the past, might have happily run up massive public sector borrowing requirements to win elections, are nowadays prevented from doing so by the hustlers of the money markets who, fearing inflation, will sell the country's currency in the wake of excessive government borrowing.

Finance ministers who try to maintain artificially inflated prices for their currencies via mechanisms such as the European Exchange Rate Mechanism also see their currencies dumped when the market decides that their pretensions are too damaging to be sustainable.

The intensely nomadic nature of these capital flows, when billions of dollars, yen and Deutschmarks are traded daily, has had some notable effects as when the UK government—pledged to hold the pound sterling to DM2.80—saw its economic policy torpedoed by international currency traders selling so many pounds that the UK government had to devalue.

With governments' economic policies already in the hands of international money traders, it seems likely that global capitalism will dictate that industrial policy goes the same way. Governments will have to pursue industrial policies which attract the investments of multinational companies, or see their unemployment situation worsen and their stock of taxpayers diminished.

Under the new nomadic financial and industrial structures, governments are going to become about the only bodies which cannot be nomadic. They will be stuck with their regions of influence while citizens and companies are going to enjoy more and more freedom to go where they want. This could well erode the powers of government in relation to the multinationals.

If this is to happen, it will take some time. Historically, companies have derived considerable benefits from being located in the countries in which they were founded. It is difficult to think of Philips without its connections with the Dutch government, or to think of Alcatel without its ties to the French government, or to see Samsung as anything other than part of the Korean government/industrial nexus.

Such government/industry relationships have been a staple of the 20th century scene, based as they are on mutual favours such as local procurement contracts, subsidised R&D, and protected markets in return for employment, taxes and social stability. But, strong as they have been, these relationships may not survive the full impact of nomadic multinationals.

Naturally, nomadic multinationals are a force acting against the natural desire of governments to support their domestic companies. They work to establish conditions on which they can compete in any market in the world, and that goes against the interests of local companies trying to protect local markets.

However, today the power of companies operating in many markets is growing inordinately because of the sheer number of new markets to be supplied. There has never been a time in history when so many new markets have suddenly emerged simultaneously. As a result of the almost global consensus that democratic capitalism is the best way to run an economy, the proliferation of new potential markets from Vladivostok to Cape Horn (via the Cape of Good Hope) has exploded.

For instance, Latin America is now expected to boom on the back of almost continent-wide acceptance of the principles under which the multinationals can invest: privatisation, free trade, acceptable rates of taxation (low) and freedom to raise capital.

In Mexico, Chile, Argentina, Paraguay, Uruguay, Venezuela, Bolivia, Peru and Ecuador there are some 400 million consumers of whom a relatively large proportion are young (in contrast to many of the mature democracies) and keen to earn and spend money on the consumer lifestyle which they see beamed in from satellite TV systems.

The greatest magnet for the multinationals is China which, while not adopting democratic capitalism, has gone for a kind of socialist capitalism. The economic figures for China are extraordinary and largely guesswork but, by some estimates, it is already the world's third largest economy behind the USA and Japan.

Per capita annual income is still very low, estimated by the Chinese government at $680 in urban areas and $180 in rural areas, but with 1200 million citizens the collective purchasing power is huge. When car ownership in China goes from 1% to 5% of the population the world car market will double! That is the kind of effect the headlong growth of China's economy is having on the rest of the world.

Urged on by the lifestyle programmes and advertisements of the 'China Star' satellite TV system—which carries mainly Western programming to over 30 million Chinese—the population is indulging a long-suppressed appetite for consumer goods. At current double-digit growth rates, the size of China's economy should double every eight years, which means it could overtake the size of the American economy in the first half of the next century.

The World Bank estimates that by 2020, China will be the world's largest economy followed by the US, Japan, India, Indonesia, Germany, South Korea, Thailand, France and Taiwan. That doesn't mean the Chinese will have the same standard of living as the Americans, but it does mean that the world's multinational companies cannot ignore China as a region in which to invest, manufacture and sell. China's potential draws them like bees to honey.

Fuelling all this is the Chinese government's unremitting drive to build infrastructure. For instance, by 2002 China plans to build 25 new airports; new telephone lines are being put in at the rate of over 10 million a year—equivalent to establishing a new American regional operator (a 'Baby Bell') every year; massive amounts of new electricity generating capacity are being built; and there are plans to build 25,000 miles of highway over the next 25 years.

Inflation is becoming a problem; tax-gathering is a severe problem; but, barring some awful political upheaval, the enthusiasm for capitalism among the Chinese is now an unstoppable force.

China's recent economic growth, averaging 9.8% CAGR since 1979 according to Chinese government statistics, is the same rate as that by which the economies of Japan, Korea and Taiwan grew in their periods of fastest growth. Not only is China an irresistible lure to foreign companies, it is irresistible to foreign tourists—foreigners are expected to be spending $10 billion a year on tourism in China by the end of the decade.

It's not just Latin America and China that have recently taken to capitalism in a major way. Vietnam, with its 70 million potential consumers, is showing its economic form by becoming the world's third largest exporter of rice (after the USA and Thailand) and is industrialising with the help of large investments from Taiwan, Hong Kong, France, Australia, Japan and Britain.

The Asian Tigers—Korea, Taiwan, Hong Kong and Singapore—continue to grow apace and Malaysia, Indonesia and the Philippines look like joining them. India with its 800 million consumers and an established, fast-growing middle-class is trying to extend its industries, particularly in high technology.

Add in the countries of the former East European bloc—Russia, Poland, Hungary, Bulgaria, Rumania, the Czech and Slovak Republics, Estonia, Latvia and the Ukraine with a collective 430 million consumers—and the sheer number of new regions where companies must consider setting up new operations or new offices is mind-boggling.

As in the days of the British Empire, when the slogan was 'trade follows the flag' or, more bluntly, trade follows the battleground successes of the Redcoats, nowadays trade is following the political successes of capitalism.

In the wake of the fall of the Berlin Wall, the collapse of Soviet communism, the partial adoption of capitalism in China, the NAFTA accords and the almost universal acceptance of capitalism, new trading opportunities are proliferating.

Governments, anxious not to miss out on the growth of their neighbours, vie for the investment of the multinationals, which strike increasingly favourable deals with governments as they spread their wings further afield. And as they spread, so their powers to influence the policies of governments increase.

It seems like an unstoppable spiral which will spawn more nomadic professionals to manage and service these far-flung industrial empires. In order to make their rootless existence tolerable—even pleasurable—they will be demanding more and more sophisticated tools and information systems.

As they travel the world, the mobile professionals will increasingly rub shoulders with another group of nomads whose numbers are also growing—tourists. There were 560 million of them in 1995, says the World Tourism Organisation (WTO), and their numbers are expected to rise to 660 million by the end of the decade. The worldwide growth figure is 5.6% a year, though there are large regional fluctuations.

Tourism to some Asian destinations has been growing by prodigious leaps—China by nearly 50% in 1994, Indonesia by nearly 40%, Thailand by over 30%, the Philippines by 23% and Hong Kong by nearly 20%.

Spending on tourism, not counting ancillary services which boost the figure ten times, amounted to over $370 billion in 1995, says the WTO, a figure which has grown at 12.6% per year for a decade. Added to that figure should be transportation costs of over $55 billion.

Air travel takes a large and increasing proportion of that figure. On a worldwide basis, 47% of all world travellers reached their destinations by air, though there are significant regional fluctuations. In Europe only a third arrived by air, in Africa 39%, in America half, and in eastern Asia and the Pacific—the highest growth market for tourism—the figure was 58% by plane.

The sheer scale of the tourism business makes it a very attractive commercial proposition for anyone who can provide a useful service for the industry. And there is such a service that new technology will shortly be providing—a replacement for travel agents.

What happens today when you go into a travel agent's office? The first thing, after you've said what you want, is that the agent looks up on his computer the availability of holidays in that destination, the flight dates and times, and the cost.

Nowadays, anyone linked to the Internet can get the same service. Effectively that puts the travel agent out of the loop for anyone who can work the Internet. Fortunately for travel agents, relatively few people can access the Internet at the moment. But their numbers will grow.

Currently, anyone with a PC, a modem and Internet access can call up exactly the same information as a travel agent and can book his holiday over the Internet. He may not yet be able to pay for it over the Internet, but it is possible now to make a separate phone call and pay by credit card.

So the travel agent could become a figure of the past as everyone gets a personal travel agent on their desk via their PC. Of course, with a Complete Nomadic Toolset and a digital wireless telephone network like the GSM system in Europe, it will be possible to adjust your travel arrangements while you're sitting in an inflatable armchair in the hotel swimming pool sipping a Daiquiri.

That Europe will be first to be able to offer such a service— because it is the first region to have a digital wireless network—is appropriate, because by far the largest proportion of foreign tourism comes to Europe. Half of all the world's tourists come to Europe, and 60% of all tourist revenues are spent in Europe. Europe has been the number one tourist destination for 35 years, says the WTO, although Europe's share has declined since 1960 when it attracted 72.5% of all tourists and 56.8% of all tourist revenues.

The second favourite tourist destination is America with about 20% of both tourists and tourist revenues. Asia is third largest with 15% of the tourists and 18% of the revenues. Africa is fourth with about 3.5% of the tourists and less than 2% of the revenues, and the Middle East is the only other sizeable destination with 1.5% of the tourists and 1% of the revenues.

Perhaps the most significant trend spotted by the WTO is that people are preferring to spend their money on tourism rather than on more traditional outlets for spending, such as manufactured goods and services.

The value of international tourism represents 8% of the value of total world exports of goods. However, when it comes to comparing tourism with the service industries, the picture is much more dramatic.

The WTO estimates that, in the mid 1990s, the average value of international tourism has grown faster than world exports of all commercial services, and international tourism now represents 30% of the value of the total world export of services. That is a very considerable testament to the nomadic urge. If this is how people are increasingly wanting to spend their money, nomadism is going to be an explosive trend of the 21st century.

Driving it will be the ever-increasing level of salaries in the developed world, and the very large numbers of people who are becoming attuned to the consumer way of life in China, Latin America, India, South-East Asia and Eastern Europe. Together those two forces could boost the number of travellers to quite extraordinary proportions.

Providing this flood of itinerants with their needs is going to be a major concern of all global businesses, whether high-tech or low-tech, whether supplying services or goods. The purchasing power of 560 million nomadic consumers is not trivial.

For the past ten years, tourism has shown steady rather than spectacular growth. The tourist trade uses a measure of activity based on tourist 'arrivals'. By this measure—based on numbers of tourists reaching destinations—tourism has increased by 5.6% per year for the last ten years. However, these growth figures could be made to look paltry in the next century when the Chinese (1.2 billion people), the East Europeans (430 million), the Indians (800 million) and the Latin Americans (400 million) start to find tourism affordable on a mass basis. A facility which has been so long denied will be all the more attractive when it becomes available.

Another group of people are increasingly hitting the tourist trail—the retired. In the mature Western democracies—North America, Japan, Europe—the population is 'greying', with an increasing proportion made up of retired people.

For instance, in North America it is expected that more than a quarter of the population will be over the age of 55 by the year 2010. A good many will be fit, energetic people with a decent pension and time on their hands. The likelihood is that they will spend an increasing proportion of it travelling.

The same sort of proportions of the retired are expected in Germany and Japan, and the foreign buying power of a Japanese or German pension is considerable, which should make a nomadic lifestyle all the more attractive to retirees from those countries.

The retired can naturally take much longer holidays than the employed, and there are organisations in the UK that offer low-season holidays of up to six-months' duration in some tourist resorts which can be less expensive than the costs that would be incurred in staying at home.

A large proportion of the retired own a home and are increasingly joining home-swap clubs where they can live for a while in someone else's house while the owners come and live in their house. Home-swapping is an inexpensive way of getting to live in another country and makes increasing sense to the retired who want all the comforts of home when they are travelling. Home-swaps are arranged on the basis of parity of accommodation, so that the houses involved are broadly of the same type.

By the time most of the retired leave work, they are usually well travelled and will be looking for new places to go. Many are keen to go to unusual places and so act as a catalyst for the travel industry to spread its services wider.

The young are another fast-growing group of travellers—as the subway systems of major cities will testify with the summer in-fluxes of backpackers. Subsidised by government schemes, by special fares, by low-cost youth accommodation, and not least by their parents, the young increasingly roam the world in their col-lege vacations. The earlier the travel bug bites these youngsters, the more they are likely to find travel a routine pastime as they get older. The chances are that we are bringing up a younger genera-tion that will travel more extensively than we now do.

For the employed, tourist travel is also increasing but in a dif-ferent way. Constrained by the demands of jobs and families, their tourism tends to be short-stay but more intensive. In Europe, with 20–25 paid holiday days a year becoming the industrial norm, it is not uncommon for industrial workers to take three foreign holi-days a year plus a number of weekend breaks away from home.

If Asia follows a similar model, that will be a big catalyst for increased tourism. In Japan, working hours are gradually being shortened, though both there and in Europe some politicians and industrialists are calling for cutbacks to workers' entitlements.

But even if Asia does not adopt the European working model, it is an inescapable fact that more people are getting richer in Asia faster than at any time in history. And experience shows that once people are rich enough to own their home and a car—and that is becoming possible for millions—they then start to think about foreign holidays.

So it would seem that there is a nomadic urge in the human heart and that more and more people are becoming rich enough to indulge it. The old and the young are travelling because they have time on their hands; the employed are travelling to get a break from busy lives; the business professional is travelling to keep up with the ever-expanding arena of international business life.

This explosion in travel has not been caused by technology—but technology is, as always, an amplifier of change. By removing some of the inconveniences of travel—dislocation from our sources of information and entertainment, loss of contact with friends and colleagues, feelings of loss of control—technology can provide people with the same degree of contact, communication and control as they have at their offices or homes.

When technology can deliver all that, then it may well amplify the current trend to travel. From the extensive, but sporadic, nomadism of today, technology's spur could turn nomadism into a mainstream lifestyle.

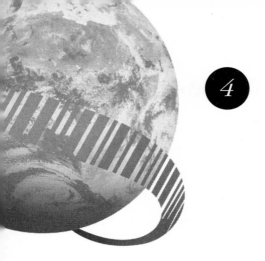

THE INCREDIBLE SHRINKING
TRANSISTOR

'There is no reason anyone would want a
computer in their home.'
Ken Olsen, Chairman and President,
Digital Equipment Corp., 1977

H ow do you predict the future of technology? Despite
Olsen's famous fallacy quoted above, nowadays it's actually rather simple.

And pretty dramatic. If the car industry had made the same
progress as the microelectronics industry in the last 50 years,

a Rolls-Royce would do a million mph, half a million mpg and would cost less than it costs to park it.

There are lots of predictions in this book. The main one is that the Complete Nomadic Toolset is only a few years away. How can we say that?

It's because the pace of technology evolution has been predictable for the past 35 years and is thought to be predictable for the next couple of decades.

All because of 'The Incredible Shrinking Transistor'.

The transistor is the basic building block of electronic technology. That's because it is the best method for representing the ones and zeroes of binary language. Why? Because the transistor's a fast, cheap switch—able to be turned on and off. When on, it can be a 1; when off, it can be a 0.

You can use 1s and 0s to store any type of 'information', whether a photograph, a piece of music, a film, video, speech, text words, drawings or whatever. And once any of these information types has been transformed into the 1s and 0s of binary language, it can be stored on a hard disc or on a chip and squirted down a telephone line or through the air.

Transferring information into the 1s and 0s of binary language is commonly called making it 'digital'—literally turning it into digits. 'Digital' has become the ubiquitous high-tech buzzword of the 90s.

Because the transistor is the cheapest and most efficient way of physically representing those digits, the transistor is the basic building block for all electronics products. And the great thing about the transistor is that it shrinks. This shrinking is behind the unstoppable progress of the electronics industry during the second half of the 20th century. It is the reason why a computer has shrunk from a roomful to a lapful in 50 years.

The transistor is now 50 years old—it was born on Christmas Eve 1947 at AT&T's Bell Laboratories in New Jersey. What has driven the electronics industry to be the second largest manufacturing industry on the planet is the transistor's ability to be miniaturised apparently endlessly. For instance, Bell Labs' transistor was about the size of a thumbnail. Today, one billion transistors fit into the same space.

The reason why the pace of technology can be predicted is that, for the last 30 years, the rate at which the transistors shrink has been predictable. This has been the case ever since the invention of the chip which is simply a collection of transistors on a single piece of silicon.

One of the pioneers of chip technology, Dr Gordon Moore, Chairman of the world's largest chip company, Intel, observed in 1965 that the number of transistors that could be put on a chip would double every year. In 1975 he amended that prediction to doubling every two years. And so it has gone on—a process known in the chip industry as 'Moore's Law'.

The key element in Moore's Law, however, is that this doubling of transistor capacity has been achieved without any significant increase in production cost. Consequently, over the last 40 years, the cost of a transistor has dropped ten million fold. 'Today one can buy a four megabit DRAM (a chip for storing information) with well over four million transistors on the chip for less than the cost of one transistor in 1960', observed Dr Moore in 1995.

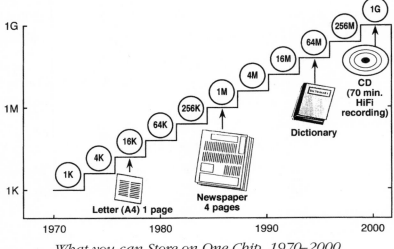

What you can Store on One Chip, 1970–2000

Since 1960, the progress of the electronics industry has been bound up with the number of transistors that could be put on one chip. By the end of the 60s, technologists could put a few hundred transistors on a chip, by the end of the 70s a few thousand, by the end of the 80s a few million, and in 1995 the first billion-transistor chips were made.

With 100 or so transistors you can't do very much, but with a few thousand you can make a simple electronic product like a calculator or a digital watch, and with about 100 million you can make a modern personal computer.

By squeezing more and more of those transistors onto each chip, you need fewer and fewer chips to make a product. And when you get down to one chip for a product, you get a very cheap product.

That is why calculators and watches were the first electronic products to be reduced to the status of Christmas stocking-fillers. Because they needed only a few thousand transistors, and because that many transistors could be put on one chip by the end of the 70s, they became the first mass-production, single-chip products.

Calculators are a good example of the power of chip technology. Back in the 1930s, full-size mechanical calculators had cost about the same as two ordinary cars. By the 1950s, electro-mechanical calculators were being made and sold for about the same price as one car.

Then, in the 1960s, chips started to be used in calculators. By 1971 the cost of a basic four-function (add, subtract, multiply, divide) calculator had dropped to $100. In 1972 it dropped to $50. By 1975 it had dropped to $20, by 1977 $14, and by 1978 $11.

Calculators shrank not only in price but also in size. Between the 1960s and the 1990s, the size of a calculator dropped from typically 70,000 cubic centimetres to 3 cubic centimetres. That was a dramatic manifestation of the effects of Moore's Law and the economies of scale derived from mass-manufacturing chips. Once all the calculator's functions could be squeezed onto a chip then the only further costs that could be driven down were those of the screen, buttons and plastic casing. So calculators reached a minimum manufacturing cost level and their prices have been pretty static ever since.

The same process happened in the early days of the PC. For instance, IBM's first PC was built in 1981 using 200 chips. Ten years later a computer with the same performance could be made by using six chips. Each memory chip in the 1981 PC contained 64,000 transistors (plus an additional 5% for control functions) and could therefore hold 64,000 binary digits (0s and 1s), known as 'bits' of information. That's about enough to store a three-page letter.

In 1996 the first commercial computers were being built using memory chips containing 64 million transistors and so able to store 64 million bits of information—enough to hold a dictionary.

The storage capacity of chips has been doubling every two years. Every three years a new generation of memory, which has four times the storage capacity of the previous generation, has been put on the market.

However, producing better and better electronic products is not just about storing more and more information in the same space for the same cost. It's also a matter of handling the information faster. Clearly the faster a computer works, the more work it can do in a given time.

The chip which defines how fast the machine works is the microprocessor. Nowadays the speed at which microprocessors work is increasing at an amazingly rapid pace (Chapter 6 includes a description of the galloping micro).

The measure of performance of electronics products like calculators and PCs is the number of 'instructions' (i.e. tasks) they can perform in a second. The first calculators could process about 1,000 instructions per second (called '1 KIPS'); the first PCs had a processing capability of one million instructions per second (1 MIPS) and, by the year 2000, High Street computers are expected to be capable of 1,000 million instructions per second (1 GIPS).

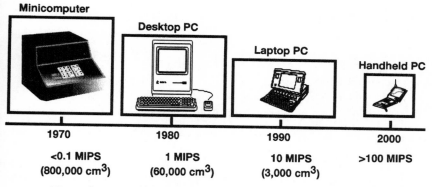

Minicomputer	Desktop PC	Laptop PC	Handheld PC
1970	1980	1990	2000
<0.1 MIPS	1 MIPS	10 MIPS	>100 MIPS
(800,000 cm³)	(60,000 cm³)	(3,000 cm³)	

How the Incredible Shrinking Transistor Changed the Computer, 1970–2000

It took 15 years to go from 1 KIPS to 1 MIPS and it will take another 15 years to go from 1 MIPS to 1 GIPS. In other words, microelectronics capability is increasing by three orders of magnitude every 15 years.

One reason for the escalation in microprocessor performance is the incredible shrinking transistor. That's because the smaller the transistors are, the closer they are packed together on the chip; and the closer the transistors are packed together, the less distance there is between them for the electrons to travel around the chip's circuitry; and the faster the electrons whizz around the chip's circuitry, the faster the microprocessor works.

There are also a number of other reasons which are currently greatly contributing to the pace of evolution of microprocessors and these are described in Chapter 6.

As the number of transistors per chip increases, so the number of functions each chip can do increases. But the cost of production of the chip remains about the same. This is why the High Street shopper expects electronic products to improve every year for the same price as the old ones. The last couple of decades have seen some astonishing progress:

- Colour TVs, video recorders, video cameras, laser printers, fax machines, scanners and mobile phones have been reduced from luxury items to commodities.
- Radios, cameras, calculators, watches and clocks have been reduced from commodity items to Christmas stocking-fillers.
- The ability to reduce all these products to a single, pocketable item is within sight.

These trends are simply explained. In 1970 the chip industry could make a chip incorporating 1,000 transistors. In 1997 it could make a chip with 64 million transistors. Both chips cost nearly the same.

This is the underlying force that has driven the electronics industry for the past 50 years. The force gives the industry the potential for a 100% improvement in the price/performance ratio of its products every two years.

The operation of Moore's Law means that, roughly speaking, either the cost of an electronic product should halve every two years, or the product's capabilities should double every two years for the same cost.

That is why the High Streets are constantly upgrading their electronic products. Printers move from black and white to colour; PCs double in speed every year or so; telephones add automatic answering, copying and faxing capabilities.

Few of the world's High Street shoppers may have heard of Moore or his law, but all of them expect electronic goods to decline in price, or to keep improving for the same price.

In chip-intensive products like PCs and mobile phones, the value of the chips can represent as much as 30% of the production cost of the end product. In these products we get either very rapid price falls or very rapidly increasing capabilities. The Complete Nomadic Toolset will be this kind of chip-intensive product. That is why, on general Moore's Law price/performance trends, it is possible to predict that the Toolset will become a possibility in the next ten years on normal Moore's Law doubling-up projections.

How does the doubling-up happen? Well, the 16 million-transistor chips of the mid-90s have transistors half a millionth of a metre in width; the 64 million-transistor chips on the market in 1997 have transistors one-third of a millionth of a metre in width.

Impossible, you might think. How do you get four times more transistors onto the same sized chip if you don't halve their size? And a reduction from a half to a third of a millionth of a metre is not a reduction by half. The answer is that the size of the chips is always getting bigger.

That's because continuing improvements in the purity of the silicon allow the use of bigger squares of silicon for each chip. Since maybe 200 square chips will be made on a round piece of silicon (called a 'wafer'), the determining factor in the size of each square is the presence or absence of defects in the silicon.

The fewer defects there are in the silicon of each wafer, the bigger the square you can safely use for making each chip without running the risk of it having a defect in the material which will make the chip faulty. So increasing silicon purity allows chips to get slightly bigger with each generation, allowing the chip companies to quadruple the numbers of transistors on each chip without actually having to halve the transistor size with every generation.

Together the effect of smaller transistors and larger chip sizes combine to give us a regular doubling in capability every couple of years. The transistor size reduction contributes about two-thirds of this increase in capability and the larger chip area contributes the other third. That is to say, the transistor size reduces by 60% every two years, providing a density increase of 2.8 times, and the chip area increases 1.4 times every two years contributing the rest of the doubling effect.

So that's how it's done and is continuing to be done. Chips with 256 million transistors in them, expected on the commercial market in 1999, will have transistors which are 0.2–0.25 millionths of a metre in width. Billion-transistor chips which are expected on the market in 2003 will have transistors which are 0.1–0.15 millionths of a metre wide.

We've already seen these quarter-billion and billion-transistor chips. That's because laboratory samples of chips are made years before they appear on the market. Prototype 256-million transistor chips were in existence in laboratories in 1993, some six years before they are expected to be seen on the market. Billion-transistor chips were first seen at a technical conference in 1995, eight years before they are expected to become available on the commercial market. The first four-billion-transistor chips were seen at a technical conference in 1997.

It used to be the case that the latest chips always obsoleted older chips, but that is happening less and older chips are staying on the market for longer and longer. For instance, in 1997 the first 64 million-transistor chips appeared in the market while the 16 million-transistor chips were in mass production and the chip being made in the highest volume was still the four million-transistor chip. And one million and 256,000-transistor chips, dating back to the early 80s, were still being made, sold and used.

That means five generations of microelectronics technology—representing 15 years of technological progress—are all on the market at the same time. This is a phenomenon which seems to be extending as chip factories get more and more expensive to build.

Not only does the cost of chip factories increase dramatically with each new chip generation, but recently the increase is rising more steeply than in the past, as shown in Table 4.1.

The enormous costs come mostly from the production machinery and the cost of filtering out dust. The production machinery accounts for 70% of the overall cost of a chip factory and that proportion is rising.

Table 4.1   Typical and projected costs of chip production factories

Number of transistors per chip	Cost of factory ($)
64,000	60,000,000
256,000	180,000,000
1,000,000	300,000,000
4,000,000	425,000,000
16,000,000	700,000,000
64,000,000	1,200,000,000
256,000,000	2,000,000,000
1,000,000,000	3,000,000,000

Source: Dataquest

Clearly it costs much more to manufacture a machine which can draw a line with a width of a tenth of a millionth of a metre than to make one which draws a line with a width of three millionths of a metre. So that 2.9 millionths of a metre in width—which represents the difference between a 64,000-transistor chip and a billion-transistor chip—costs $2,940,000,000. This is the difference in cost between a $60 million factory for 64,000-transistor chips and a $3 billion factory for billion-transistor chips.

Why does it cost so much? The reason is that, in order to make the billion-transistor chip efficiently, it will have to be made in a factory where every particle of dust larger than 0.1 millionth of a metre has to be extracted, otherwise the dust landing on the chips would create disconnections or short-circuits in the chips and most would be duds.

If you extrapolate the chip size to the size of a football field, then the 0.1 millionth of a metre transistor size corresponds to an object measuring half a millimetre on the football field. So the task in making a factory clean enough to make billion-transistor chips efficiently corresponds to removing all particles bigger than half a millimetre from a room the size of a football field!

That's one reason why the cost of building a factory to do that is expected to be over $3 billion, but the main reason is the cost of the equipment required to make these tiny structures which has been rapidly increasing to the point where equipment cost now represents between two-thirds and three-quarters of the cost of building a chip factory. So the vast sums required to make the latest chips can only be justified if the chip-makers keep on making older chips long after they are overtaken by new ones.

The ever-escalating costs, and the need to make a return on investments, could eventually slow the pace at which the electronics industry is able to miniaturise and drive down costs.

That's only a maybe. Every time there's a new shift in the technology to smaller transistors and line widths, the accountants have said that the costs are so huge that the products must be sold for more. But it hasn't happened. And for the next ten years, it is generally thought that normal 'Moore's Law' miniaturisation and cost reductions will continue. That is good news for nomads because it should give us time to develop, and cost-effectively manufacture, the Complete Nomadic Toolset.

Naturally, the smaller the transistors the fewer the chips, and the fewer the chips the smaller the equipment. Since the Complete Nomadic Toolset is an amalgam of different equipment types all miniaturised and rolled into one, the trick is to try to squeeze all its transistors into as few chips as possible.

The historical trend suggests we can predict the rate at which the price of any electronic product is going to fall, the rate at which it is going to get smaller, and the rate at which it is likely to get absorbed into another electronic product, such as combined PC/TV or fax/phone/copier/printer/answerphone.

So that's the main reason why the incredible shrinking transistor is going to deliver a Complete Nomadic Toolset within a decade.

But there is another reason: the worldwide trend in all types of communications—telephone lines, mobile telephones, radio and TV broadcasts—to move from analogue systems to digital systems.

Until recently, none of these means of communication was digital, i.e. based on the 1s and 0s of binary language. Broadcasting to

TVs or radios and making telephone calls either on a phone line or via a mobile has been done by using 'analogue' technology.

Analogue means model. Analogue electronics means taking a 'real world' phenomenon such as heat, light or sound and simulating it in an electronic model.

For instance, children find they can talk to each other using two tin cans connected by a string. The cans set up a vibration caused by speaking and the string carries the vibrations to the other can. If instead of the tin cans you use a vibrating membrane which can make an electrical model (or analogue) of those vibrations, and send them along a wire, you get a telephone.

If, instead of sending the models along a wire, you feed them into a transmitter, you can send them through the air either as a radio broadcast message intended to be picked up by many people, or as a point-to-point radio message intended to be received by only one particular person.

A good description of the technology used the following words: 'Vocal or other sounds telegraphically transmitted by causing electrical undulations similar in form to the vibrations of the air accompanying the said vocal or other sounds'. That was how Alexander Graham Bell described it in US Patent No. 174,465 granted in 1876 for his invention of the telephone.

And so it has been for 120 years. This analogue communications technology has been used for radio and TV broadcasts and phone calls. However, in the 1990s things changed rapidly. It became accepted in the developed world that it would be better to convert these analogue signals into the 1s and 0s of digital signals before sending them.

Digital has the advantages over analogue of providing more consistent quality and of allowing many more simultaneous phone calls in each frequency band of the radio spectrum—an important requirement as the world's usage of the spectrum escalates with more broadcasting channels and more mobile phones.

So, countries have begun switching to digital systems for mobile telephones and to digital broadcasts for both radio and TV.

The big digital TV front runners are expected to be the satellite broadcasters. In Europe, Canal Plus Satellite Numérique was first to get going in 1996 with a 20-channel operation, with the capacity to go to 50.

BSkyB does not want to be far behind. The German media group Leo Kirch has the Astra1E satellite launch in spring 1997 and the Astra1F in summer 1997 to bring TV and multimedia services to German viewers.

In contrast to digital broadcast services, digital wireless telephone services are already well underway. Seventy-one countries now have digital wireless networks and another 13 are building them. In 1995 and 1996, the USA auctioned off licences for digital wireless networks and raised over $16 billion from budding network operators.

This is very good news for the potential nomad because every type of information he's going to need—pictures, text, video, music, voice, etc.—will all come to him via these networks in exactly the same form—a stream of 1s and 0s. This has a particularly helpful effect on the process of merging all the different electronic product types because it will mean that a lot of the electronics can be combined instead of duplicated.

For instance, in the early versions of the PC/TVs you get an analogue TV in the same casing as a digital PC. When the TV is also digital, the electronics inside a PC/TV will be considerably simplified, take up a lot less space and be much cheaper.

When all the means of communication (mobile phones, wired phones, satellite phone calls, radio broadcast, TV broadcast, satellite broadcast) and all the different types of 'information' (photos, film, video, text, voice, music, etc.) are in the 1s and 0s of digital technology, the merging of equipment types becomes much simpler.

With the digitisation of all forms of electronics activity—TV and radio broadcasting, TV receivers, telephone calls both wired and wireless, fax machines, computers, etc.—the pace of merging equipment types will accelerate.

For instance, digitisation is going to mean that TV sets and computers will become much more similar electronically, because both computers and TVs will be dealing with streams of digitised data—the only difference being that the computer gets its stream from a disc or a chip whereas the TV gets its stream from a broadcast transmission.

When both TV broadcasts and TV sets are all-digital, then the electronic innards of a TV will look much the same as those of a computer.

Both a computer and a TV will be capable of handling all kinds of digital information whether it is coming in from a disc, a chip, an audio or video broadcast, a satellite broadcast, a video tape, a telephone line, a wireless telephone, or a fax machine.

This could be confusing to the traditional TV set manufacturers and computer manufacturers who won't know which business they are in! For the microelectronics boys, however, it represents a marvellous opportunity.

The microelectronics industry is exploiting the opportunity by producing chip-sets which can add all these different types of digitised information flow to the computer. These chip-sets start off large and expensive—say six or seven chips costing $2,000— and get cheaper every year as it becomes possible to do the same things on fewer chips.

Chip-sets first for video, then for telephone, fax, TV and mobile phone will all come out, allowing you to hook these sources of information on to your computer.

Eventually every new function to be added to the computer will be done on one chip and then, whatever that function is, it will be so cheap to add on to a computer that it will become a standard feature on all computers.

The result of this gradual progress to computer/TVs which do everything possible with digitised information is that there will be a merging of all the various machines which at the moment handle their own specific types of information.

Looking back from the first decade of the 21st century we'll be amazed at all the different equipment types we used to have in the 1990s—printers, faxes, answering machines, phones, computers, TVs, etc. What will have happened between then and now is that ubiquitous digitisation will have reduced them all to a single machine.

The progress towards the all-singing all-dancing all-purpose machine will be gradual. It is possible to buy a chip set on a card costing under $1,000 which connects a telephone to a

Lifestyle: Today—Multiple Machines; Future—One Machine

personal computer allowing it to receive video and audio data down the telephone line, effectively turning the computer into a videophone.

The chip-set will halve in number of chips and cost every couple of years until it is down to one or two chips and cheap enough to be included in every computer as a standard feature.

The same will happen for video. First an expensive chip-set will be sold as an additional unit allowing you to plug a video into the computer. The price will come down and then, when adding video to a computer takes only one or two chips, the feature will be incorporated into computers as a standard feature.

Again for TV cameras. Chip-sets for plugging these directly into the computer so that the computer can receive transmissions sent from a TV camera or a camcorder will be sold as add-ons. Then these chip-sets will get reduced to a single chip, will be mass-manufactured, made affordable to all and turned into an everyday feature of all computers.

When digital broadcasts become sufficiently widespread, chips will be made that will connect a computer to a TV aerial to receive TV programmes.

For functions like faxing, printing or copying, chip-sets connect the fax machine and the photocopier to the computer, allowing a computer user to send the document on his screen to a fax machine for transmission or to a photocopier to be copied.

Chips which link up the computer, the fax and the photocopier were 1995 products that first appeared as chip-sets on boards that slotted into a computer. They will rapidly decline in price until it needs only one or two chips to do the job whereupon they'll be put inside the computer as a standard feature.

The result of all these moves is that the various equipment types we use today will all merge into each other. For instance, two machines whose functions look like merging indistinguishably are the fax and the printer.

When printers are connected up to the telephone system they will be able to print out from any location, and with faxes printing on plain paper with letter quality and in colour there will be no difference in function between a fax and a printer. They will become a single machine.

And since the single machine will be dealing with a single type of information flow—the 1s and 0s of digital language—it will be able to take on board spoken messages and video messages as well as written messages. So the merged fax/printer adds to itself the functions of the videophone and the telephone.

Meanwhile, pocket telephones will also be taking on more of the functions of other machines—able to send and receive faxes, for example. In order to send faxes they will need some of the features of computers such as word processing, and since they will need large screens for word processing it will be a short step to add on TV. So the portable telephone becomes a phone/fax/computer/TV.

At the same time, portable computers are expanding to grab the functions of the telephone. First computers got plugged into the telephone network; now they are tied into wireless networks; later they will be picking up video and TV. So the computer also becomes a computer/phone/fax/TV.

The result is that a TV becomes like a computer, a computer becomes like a telephone, a fax machine becomes like a printer, and a telephone becomes like a computer/fax/printer/TV.

Eventually everything will merge into a single, seamless unit— all brought about by the shrinking transistor driving down cost and size while digitisation reduces complexity.

Whether it's a single, seamless unit, a videophone or a computer with videophone capability, there is one other function all these will need: the ability to *transmit* TV pictures as well as see them.

Already the electronics of a TV camera can be compressed onto a single chip making the electronics cheap. Adding this capability to computers/phones/faxes/TVs or whatever is not a big issue on cost grounds.

In the digital age, a machine will not have to deal any differently with, say, a radio broadcast coming over the air and a video being transmitted down a phone line—both are just a stream of 1s and 0s to the machine. Similarly, information coming off a PC hard disc will seem, to the machine, just the same as information coming in from a mobile telephone. All the machine has to handle is a stream of 1s and 0s, no matter what information type is being dealt with and no matter how it is being sent.

So the twin thrusts of the Incredible Shrinking Transistor and digitisation are pushing electronics products unstoppably towards size reduction, lower cost and merging product types.

Moore's Law makes the pace of that progress predictable. During the next ten years, the technology trends say that the industry will deliver the affordable, pocketable Complete Nomadic Toolset.

THE COMMUNICATIONS
REVOLUTION

'The shrinking world has shrunk'.
John Golding, Chairman Hewlett-Packard UK, 1996

THE title of this chapter sounds complicated until you appreciate that it boils down to one thing—the speed with which you
can communicate over the public telephone systems. And the
only thing worth saying about it is that the speed and capacity are
increasing.

That would make for a short chapter. But it would also be
misleading because the interesting thing is not the change but the

mind-boggling rate and scale of the change—and the implications that has for lifestyles.

That's because the enormous increase in the capability of the existing telephone wires is going to make it possible to send things along them which have never been sent before. So far we've just used telephones for talking to people. Soon we'll be able to send every type of digital information—which means any type of information—videos, photos, drawings, music and books.

Nowadays you cannot plug your camcorder into your phone jack and send the pictures to auntie in Australia; you cannot, in your living room, hold a six-way phone conversation with video pictures of all the participants; you can't dial up the Blockbuster Video store and have a movie transmitted to you down the phone line.

But you will. All it needs is for the communications links to your home—the telephone wires connecting up your telephone—to be able to carry more 1s and 0s of binary information than they currently do.

The frustrating thing is that the existing wires could carry enough bits of data per second to do all those things now, if only the telephone network operators were prepared to make cur-rently existing technology available to us all inexpensively.

Bear in mind the sheer diversity of types of link which go to make up the telecommunications network. Into your home, com-ing through the outside wall is usually what's known in the tele-coms trade as a 'twisted pair'—copper wires which carry phone calls. They are the final link in the telecommunications network.

Out in the street, the twisted pair connects up to either another copper cable ('coaxial cable') or to a fibre-optic cable. A fibre-optic cable is made of glass or plastic down which flashes of light carry the messages instead of, as in copper cable, a series of electrons running along the wires. The 'fibre' or 'co-ax' cables connect up to the local telephone exchange.

Between one telephone exchange and another telephone exchange, the cable connections are increasingly fibre-optic because of its larger carrying capacity (bandwidth).

Between countries, the connections are sometimes by cable where this is convenient, for instance where it can be put under the sea, and sometimes by wireless links, such as via satellites. Telecommunications satellites are purely orbiting telephone exchanges.

From these satellites, signals are beamed up from telephone exchanges and beamed back down to other telephone exchanges. And, of course, from the exchange they are sent along cables to the streets, then up from your street along twisted pairs into your home.

But that's only the start of it. Alongside this sort of system which is operated by the likes of the former national telephone systems operators—AT&T of the US, BT of the UK, Japan, France Télécom, etc.—are the wireless networks of the mobile phone operators.

Some of these mobile phone networks are of the so-called 'cellular' type. As the name suggests, these are built like honeycombs with a transmitter/receiver station covering an area (a 'cell') which interlocks with other cells. This means that you can drive your car from cell to cell while making a continuous (hopefully!) phone call with the signal from your phone being picked up and passed on from cell to cell. The mobile networks then feed the signals from the mobile phone into the ordinary fixed line telephone network which can relay them around the world.

There are already some specialised systems which allow mobile phones direct access to satellites such as via the Inmarsat satellite constellation—but these involve very cumbersome, heavy equipment (15–16 pounds) and are costly.

However, hoping to bring satellite mobile communications to the masses are six proposals, some at an advanced stage, for putting up constellations of satellites capable of providing self-contained, affordable, global networks which can be accessed by pocketable telephones: Iridium, Loral-Qulacomm, Ellipsat, TRW, Teledesic and Constellation.

Satellite systems are particularly needed in large, sparsely in-habited countries like mid-America, China or Russia where it is not cost-effective to set up cellular systems or to bury vast quantities of copper or fibre-optic cable in the ground.

Fibre, co-ax, twisted pair, cellular radio, satellites—that is the nervous system of the Internet. They comprise the connections which carry signals around the globe. All have the potential to carry any kind of signal whether it is a conversation, text message, music, graphics, a photograph or video.

Added to all this telecoms communications structure, the 21st century nomad will have all the benefits of broadcast TV, both terrestrial and satellite. And with TV carrying extensive information services such as Prestel and Teletext, the nomad is likely to be in little danger of information starvation. It all depends on getting the technologies we already have out into the field and working.

Although the technology problems involved in sharply increasing the capacity of public telephone lines have been solved, they are not being implemented because governments, network operators and service providers are squabbling over economic consequences, including how they can best make money from the new capabilities.

The new capabilities apply to all the standard public communications links—wireless networks for mobile phones, the copper wires which come into our homes, and the fibre-optic cables which are increasingly making up the 'trunk' routes from one telephone exchange to another.

The difference between what we have and what we could have is stunning. What we have is copper wires capable of delivering a maximum of 28,800 bits of data in a second. The latest state-of-the-art in a laboratory is fibre-optic cable delivering 1,000,000,000,000 bits per second (one terabit per second).

While there is little chance of seeing the latter rate of transmission in commercial form for maybe 20 years, it is possible already to increase the 28,800 bits per second we have now to 144,000 bits per second, and to a few million bits per second during this decade. The hope has to be that the technology will be made available to everyone reasonably inexpensively.

The makers of the technology can provide it inexpensively, because they can reduce it to silicon chips which, once made in volume, quickly reduce in cost (by roughly 30% per year). The problem is whether the network operators will provide the chips to customers inexpensively or whether they will impose huge mark-ups.

The route they take will determine whether there's a quick customer take-up—leading to a rapid increase in use for the entire network—or whether the take-up will be slow, having little effect on generating new services which can be put onto the network.

That's because the increases in capability are going to make a lot of new services possible on the telephone networks. For instance, take a look at the effect of the increase in capability from 28,800 bits per second to several million bits per second. What could that do in practice? Look at a couple of examples: the time it takes to send a book or a video down a telephone line.

Since it requires 16 million bits to store a copy of the book *Gone with the Wind*, it would today, at 28,800 bits per second, take about ten minutes to send it down a phone line to another computer. But increase that carrying capacity to 144,000 bits per second—available to domestic users today—and it takes 2 minutes; increase it to six million bits per second—technology that could be available to domestic users in a year or two—and that reduces to two and a half seconds.

In fact it will take less than two and a half seconds because it is possible to precis digitised information so that it uses fewer bits of information storage space. These 'compression' techniques allow you to compress digitised written data by about three times.

The technique of compression is theoretically pretty simple. It involves looking for repeated patterns in the 0s and 1s of digital language and replacing those repeated patterns with a symbol. The hardware costs of doing that are dropping fast because the technology for performing the compression/decompression function can now all be put on a few chips. And once a technology is reduced to chips, it is on the chip cost decline curve of 30% cost erosion per year.

Chips which perform the compression function (and decompression at the other end) were developed in the 90s and quickly became a big market. As in other areas where chips are involved, prices of compression/decompression chips soon began to fall rapidly, making it a very affordable technology.

So instead of a 16 million bit *Gone with the Wind* we now have a compressed five million bit version which we can send down the phone line—at today's fastest commercial rate of 28,800 bits per second in about three minutes. When we have, hopefully later this decade, a rate of six million bits per second, it will take less than one second.

Now take *Gone with the Wind*—the movie. With movies the numbers start to get very big compared to text. A single frame in a video requires two million binary 1s and 0s to be stored in digital form. In a video film there are 30 frames for every second of film. So every second of video time requires 60 million bits of storage. A minute needs 3,600 million bits, an hour needs 216,000 million bits, and the three hours of *Gone with the Wind* will require 648,000 million bits to store it.

At the current rate of 28,800 bits per second, the time it takes to send 60 million bits representing a second of film time down a phone line is about half an hour. So it would take over a day to transmit a minute of video. To send the full three hours of *Gone with the Wind* would take 260 days!

Fortunately, the ability to compress video is very much higher than the ability to compress written data. Video can be compressed 30 times without losing an acceptable level of quality. The reason why the compression ratio for digitised video is 30:1 when the compression ratio for digitised words is only 3:1 is that it is not necessary to digitise the background of every video frame.

Where backgrounds do not differ much, the background information need be digitised only once and a symbol can then be used to repeat the information. For instance, if there's a three-minute shot in the video of a ship at sea, you'll have 5,400 successive frames (at 30 per second) each normally requiring two million bits of storage. But you can replace the string of 1s and 0s representing the sea and sky—which take up much of each frame—with a couple of symbols. So instead of requiring 5,400 × 2 million or 10,800 million bits to store the three-minute sequence, compression techniques could reduce the storage requirement to say 360 million bits.

The longer the background is repetitive the more it can be compressed. That makes for considerable savings in storage space.

Taking a fairly standard compression ratio of 30:1, the three-hour video of *Gone with the Wind* can be stored in 21,600 million bits. Sending this down a telephone wire at 28,800 bits per second would take about nine days.

However, when the transmission rate is increased to six million bits per second via a technology called ADSL (Asynchronous Digital Subscriber Line), then you'll be able to send a compressed digitised three hours of video down a phone line in 1 hour. That is all done using the existing copper wires coming into our homes.

Of course it would be better to use fibre-optic cables which have much greater carrying capacity than six million bits per second but, because it's an expensive proposition to dig up streets and gardens to supply new cables to homes, people concentrate on increasing the carrying capacity of the existing wires.

However, the biggest advances in communications will be coming from fibre optics. Current fibre-optic cables deliver data at 2,400 million bits per second; under development are cables capable of 5,400 million bits per second delivery, and 20,000 million bits per second cables are coming out of laboratories. As mentioned above, the highest rate reached in laboratories is the 1,000,000 million bits per second (one terabit per second or 1Tbit/sec) by Fujitsu, AT&T's Bell Labs and NTT at the Optical Fibre Conference in San Jose in February 1996.

The capabilities are increasing all the time—at a much faster rate than the network operators can utilise them by putting them into telephone systems and delivering us some benefits.

At 2,400 million bits per second, the three-hour video of *Gone with the Wind* would be transmitted in under 10 seconds. So in the course of the 1990s, the standard time taken to send three hours of video to your home could go down from 260 days to a few seconds! That is the force driving the communications revolution.

Hopefully, sometime in the future—presumably during the 21st century—the entire telephone network will be converted exclusively to use fibre optics in place of all the copper wires and electrical equipment and components. When not only the cables but the equipment in the telephone exchanges and switching stations and all the componentry will be optical, the transmission rate will be increased to 1,000,000,000,000 bits per second (one terabit per second).

The snag in all this happening is investment. Network operators may well conclude that they would be investing to put themselves out of business. For instance, when we have rates of data transmission in the thousands of millions of bits per second range, it could be difficult for the network operators to make any money.

How, for instance, do you charge for messages which are taking only a few thousandths, millionths even, of a second to deliver? Messages could be whizzing around all over the world at near-zero cost—a nightmare for network operators!

If the network operators can't see any return in it, they are not likely to invest the very large sums to install the new technologies. To invest billions to put yourself out of business is not an attractive option to most executives.

They could, of course, charge for services down the line instead of time on the line. In the UK, BT have been debarred from doing this by government because the government wants to keep the potentially lucrative market for services for the cable companies which have been undergoing the expense of installing fibre-optic cable. BT has lobbied hard against their restriction, clearly believing that service provision may become a better financial bet than running networks.

Another alternative is for governments to make the investment in the hope that it will lead to increased economic activity. But governments in the West are ideologically committed to not competing with industry and, anyway, they are all struggling with money and popularity problems. Putting billions into an 'information superhighway' is not going to be a cost-effective vote-catcher.

So, for the time being, the likelihood is that expense will dictate that the copper wires into our homes will not be replaced by fibre-optic cable, we will not get thousands of millions of bits per second carrying capacity this century (though we should get several millions of bits per second), and the most likely way in which we will see our carrying capacity increased this decade will come from increasing the speeds at which data can be carried over copper.

For instance, by installing a few silicon chips in your home plus a few more at your telephone exchange, the carrying capacity on your existing telephone line would be increased from 28,800 bits per second to 144,000 bits per second.

The service—called ISDN, standing for Integrated Services Digital Network—will work on 86% of all phone lines in the USA and 94% of all phone lines in Europe, if the chips are installed.

The attitude of the phone network operators to ISDN is interesting. For instance, although commercial technology capable of implementing ISDN has been around for 10 years, and although the cost of all the chips required is under £20 in bulk, BT only made the service available to domestic customers in 1995 and, when they did, charged a £400 installation fee and an £85 quarterly charge. Charges later reduced but they were still high in the late 1990s. That seems to be an attitude almost designed to slow the take-up of the technology and the new services it would make possible.

Even so, customers are not going to be satisfied with the quality of video delivered at ISDN's 144,000 bits per second. A minimum transmission rate for broadcast quality video is seen as two million bits per second.

However, 144,000 bits per second will give you quite a lot. For example, it gives you the ability to download and transmit very large data files at reasonable cost in terms of time on the line. That would be very useful for people working at home who need to get files off the office computer and send them back.

Another thing which 144,000 bits per second would give you is videoconferencing. Although this is possible at 28,800 bits per second the quality is poor, movements are staccato and it is only possible at all because of very high compression ratios. At 144,000 bits per second videoconferencing is of a more acceptable standard.

However, as well as ISDN, and using the same sort of technological method (a set of silicon chips at each end of the telephone line), you will soon be able to increase your 28,800 bits per second capacity to six million bits per second. The technology is called ADSL, standing for Asynchronous Digital Subscriber Line.

As with all telephone technologies the signal naturally gets weaker the further it travels, but using ADSL it is possible to send data at six million bits per second for up to 12,000 feet (3,600 metres). It is estimated that this is near enough to a trunk-line telephone cable connection to allow 80% of the developed world's 560 million people to adopt ADSL. In the UK, it would reach 92% of subscribers. If a remote terminal is installed in the network that percentage could be increased to 100%.

If you had ADSL in your home now you would be able, according to the US company Motorola, to call up four separate VHS quality videos and watch them on four separate TVs, while at the same time holding a 384,000 bits per second commercial quality videoconference and downloading text files at 128,000 bits a second—all while carrying on a telephone conversation!

The beauty of the ADSL technology is that you get very high carrying capacity without having to dig up roads and gardens to lay fibre-optic or coaxial cable. That last bit of connection to your home—called the 'local loop' or 'last mile'—is the current bottleneck holding up an explosion in communications capability. Digging up roads and gardens is so expensive and has such an unpredictable take-up from potential users that telephone network operators are reluctant to make the investment.

With a technique such as ADSL, involving merely the installation of a chip-set at the exchange and another at the customer's home, both the expense of excavation and the unpredictability of customers are bypassed. Unlike cable, if potential customers for ADSL don't want the service, it hasn't cost the network operator anything to offer it.

ADSL is clearly one way of clearing the local loop/last mile bottleneck. It has already been trialled by 30 network operators in the USA, Europe, Asia and Australia and commercial availability should not lag long behind the trials.

The ADSL technology can be upgraded. It is believed it can be stretched to give carrying capacity up to a maximum of 52 million bits per second.

The sort of thing people will want ADSL for are the ability to dial up to send movies down the telephone line; the ability to call up the contents of remotely held CD-ROMs holding video, graphics, photos, text and music; the ability to 'log on' to the Internet faster (nowadays it can take a long time to get a connection); and, lastly, the ability to connect up to a local network—such as an internal office network or an organisation's private network—from a long distance away.

These sorts of limited networks, known as Local Area Networks or LANs, have very much faster capabilities than domestic copper wiring, for two reasons: first, the quality of the cable is better; secondly, the terminals—PCs, printers, faxes or whatever—which are connected up in LANs are closer together.

So where ADSL comes in is to get rid of the frustration of having a 28,800 bits per second connection to a LAN which has a 10 million bits per second capacity. Having an ADSL link at the user's end will help to match up the capabilities of the public network with the capabilities of the LAN.

That is particularly useful for people working from home—teleworkers—who often have to download large quantities of information from the office and then send equally large amounts back to their office computer. By having an ADSL link for the local loop they can work with the office network from home as easily as if they were in the office.

LAN transmission rates are speeding ahead. The carrying capacity of LANs over the rest of the decade is expected to increase by at least ten times, giving us 100 million bits per second plus transmission rates within the next five years.

Those are the kinds of capabilities that are possible, and will be possible, over fixed communications links. However, just increasing the speed of the links doesn't complete the job. After all, the whole point of the job is to take a network that was used only for talking to people and add new functions to it like sending video, digital audio, photos, drawings, digital music and data.

As we've seen, the book of *Gone with the Wind* can be stored in five million bits. However, the video of *Gone with the Wind* needs 648,000 million bits of storage. If you were sending information made up of synchronised voice, text, graphics, music and video, then you would need the book and the video to arrive at the same time over the same communications links.

It's not just a problem getting these data streams to arrive at their destination simultaneously but also coping with a network in which different parts have very different carrying capacities.

The answer to this is a technology called ATM (Asynchronous Transfer Mode) which will take a digital data stream, break it down into segments, move it between networks with different carrying capacities and put it all back together again in the right order with the voice, video and data being delivered simultaneously.

A good thing about ATM technology is that it has been reduced to silicon chips, meaning it can be made constantly cheaper as volume demand goes up and the size of transistors goes down. So it will be an increasingly affordable technology—which is very good news because it is the key to multimedia communications over telephone lines.

If enormous effort is going into the technology of fixed communications, just as much effort, if not more, is going into wireless links. Wireless is currently the glamour side of the communications business.

How often do we see, in portrayals of life in the future, someone in a deckchair on a beach videoconferencing with work colleagues via a laptop computer? It's a beguiling vision for office-phobes and one that many people would love to see made reality.

It is possible that it will be real this decade. Certainly it has already been demonstrated—at the 1995 Geneva Telecommunications Show by Andy Grove, President of Intel. 'That application makes me covet that computer', said Grove afterwards, believing, as do many, that people will flock to buy mobile videoconferencing tools as soon as they become available.

Mobile videoconferencing is, many think, a 'killer app' in the argot of the high-tech industry, meaning an application which people will go crazy to buy—like the first spreadsheet programme, the first word-processing package or the first computer game.

But just because something is demonstrated at a technology show does not mean it's about to appear in the shops. It's salutary to remember that the first videotelephone was demonstrated at the World's Fair of 1964. And how many of us have them over 30 years later?

The problems are not problems of electronic hardware. It is possible to incorporate the electronics which will add video-conferencing to a laptop computer for around $1,000. Since this capability will be added in the form of a set of chips, the cost should drop by roughly 30% a year once videoconferencing becomes a popular application in portable computers, demand for the chips goes up, the number of chips required to do the job goes down, and the chips get established on the industry learning curve.

So the hardware is not a problem. Nor is there any technical problem in using radio to send video (after all, it is broadcast every day to hundreds of millions of TV sets). The problems start because the ideal network for mobile videoconferencing does not yet exist. Therefore it will be necessary to use existing networks. And existing digital wireless networks have their limitations.

At the moment, the only region in the world which has a wireless telephone network which is anywhere near ubiquitous is Europe. Europe has the GSM network for digital wireless communications which, with a few holes, covers most of the population. Japan and the USA have lagged behind as their governments dithered over allocating frequencies and setting technical standards for the networks.

However, in 1995 the Japanese digital wireless system, called PHS, got under way, China and India have fast-growing networks, and the Americans at last got their digital wireless services going in 1997. In the USA the four consortia who have been licensed to operate digital cellular networks have agreed to pay the US government $7.6 billion for the privilege. The consortia will start recouping that outlay only when they begin to generate revenue from phone calls.

The Americans are looking at two other standards for digital cellular besides GSM: CDMA (Code Division Multiple Access) and TDMA (Time Division Multiple Access).

So for Europe, and for more than 50 countries outside Europe which have adopted GSM, the system for mobile videoconferencing will be a GSM one. The problem with using GSM for videoconferencing is that, although capable of 14,400 bits per second, it is guaranteed to provide only 9,600 bits per second on a reliable basis.

That is simply not enough carrying capacity to send anything except an extremely poor quality picture. At 64,000 bits per second you get an acceptable quality of picture but you still get the staccato effect in any movements. Furthermore, even 64,000 bit per second mobile networks are nowhere in sight. To achieve the level of quality which you get on commercial videoconferencing you need 384,000 bits per second, and for the same quality as you get on a TV screen you need two million bits per second—and there's no mobile network in the world even considering that.

So the problems appear to be insuperable. But there is a way round it. Since videoconferencing requires only a picture of a talking head where all the background and most of the face do not change much from frame to frame, it is possible to compress the information in each frame to a far greater extent than with a normal frame in a video.

So for videoconferencing, a much higher compression ratio is usable, allowing each frame to be stored in fewer bits and so permitting a much lower bit per second carrying rate than for video. In 1995 the US approved 28,800 bits per second as a videoconferencing standard. On the face of it that doesn't help a lot because 28,800 bits per second is still above the 9,600 bits per second allowed by GSM digital wireless networks—and these are the only networks there are.

However, there is a way round this that could give us mobile videoconferencing on existing networks without having to wait for networks to start offering 28,800 bits per second transmission rates. The solution is to use three to eight GSM channels simultaneously and 'glue' them together using a piece of equipment known as a 'channel aggregator'. That way it would be possible to achieve 28,800 bits per second carrying capacity or, with eight channels, 64,000 bits per second.

According to David Heatley, Head of Mobile Systems (Future) at BT in the UK, 'It's not just an idea, it's a technological possibility'. BT reckons it will be possible this decade, and that it could even start to happen around 1998.

As with fixed-link communications, the future for wireless communications is in optical links. But, as you can imagine, it's a lot more difficult using light for wireless communications than it is in fixed-link communications where you've got a glass fibre to send the light down.

Instead of fibre-optic links, in wireless communications you're using 'free space' optics. That means using laser beams to send messages through the ether—rather like sending a Morse Code message on a sunny day using a mirror to reflect sunbeams.

Free-space optics are envisaged in the 21st century, though it could start happening in some form during this decade. Certainly network operators like BT have teams working on this kind of system. One advantage of using light for communications is that its carrying capacity is so huge that there will be no need for compression—so reception will be instantaneous and picture quality will not be degraded. A second advantage is the sheer power of lasers—a laser beam from Earth has been reflected off the Moon. A possible disadvantage, says Heatley, is that 'any pigeons getting in the way would be fricasséed instantly'.

Another possibility for wireless communications is the launch, by various consortia, of constellations of satellites to provide a brand new, global mobile telephone network. There are six of these consortia: Ellipsat, TRW, Constellation, Iridium, Loral/ Qualcomm and Teledesic. Iridium launched the first of its 66-satellite constellation in 1997 and intends to have all 66 in orbit, and a service in operation, in 1998. That will have a big effect on bringing mobile communications to those parts of the world where low population density makes cellular systems uneconomic.

That really rounds up the possible and almost possible things that are happening in communications technology. The prospects are stunning because solutions are in place for the main bottlenecks—ISDN and ADSL for the local loop, ATM for marrying up different data types in one transmission, GSM for wireless communications, and optics for the main trunk routing.

All it needs is for the investments to be made to put the new technologies in place, and for the various national telecommunications regulatory regimes to create environments which encourage their adoption.

Once adopted, these increases in data transmission capability will have huge effects on people's perception of how to use a telephone line. For one thing, it should get very much cheaper.

At the moment, time on the telephone line is still a relatively expensive commodity but two things should change that. First, the extra carrying power of the network is going to make a massive difference to communications costs.

For instance, when you can send hundreds of millions of bits of information down a phone line in a minute—a conservative estimate of capability later this decade—then people will start to use that capability because a minute of phone time costs very little.

The other reason why phone charges will drop is deregulation. Governments around the world are deregulating their telephone networks in the hope of stoking up competition.

In the UK there are a number of competitors to the former monopoly supplier BT. Ingenious ways have been found by these competitors to install new networks besides just digging up streets.

For instance, one consortium with a licence to set up a new telephone network—Energis—is draping its fibre-optic cables along the electricity pylons. Another consortium is putting them under the towpaths along the canal network; another is laying them alongside the railway network.

That's OK for the trunk routing. What remains the main problem for these operators is the local loop. How do you get the service from your trunk cable to people's homes without spending a fortune digging up streets?

If you lay a cable in the street it's very expensive, and when you ask people if they want to be connected up to it, many will say no—so it's an unpredictable, possibly profitless exercise.

If you want to use BT's wires, they may either refuse or charge you a hefty rental. There is a possibility of using the domestic electricity wiring for telephone services but not all the technical problems are solved. The problem could be solved—as they are solving it extensively in India—by using wireless communications for the local loop.

So, just as the local loop is the bottleneck for upgrading the overall capacity of the telephone system, so it is the biggest barrier to getting new competitor networks off the ground.

However, some governments in the developed world remain determined that effective competition should be introduced in the telephone network business, believing that it is the only way to get lower charges for time on the line.

Lower charges combined with big increases in the carrying capacity could provide new commercial, entertainment and educational opportunities, though people are a little woolly on exactly what these opportunities will be.

Some point to the example of the fax. The technology to make fax machines had been around for 30 years before faxes were sold in High Street shops. Until then, no one knew they wanted a fax. But, once available, they caught on very quickly and now the fax machine is a ubiquitous business tool.

Once people start to see that they can easily use a powerful new resource, and use it cheaply, then uses for it will be found, especially because many people already have the basic hardware for the electronic communications—the PC. When we add cheap, robust, easy-to-use, ubiquitous electronic communications to PCs, people could find that more useful than fax.

For instance, anyone with a product to sell that can be reduced to digital form—and in the Information Age there are an increasing number of people who have such products—will be able to deliver the product cheaply anywhere in the world. It will be very much cheaper to link several people together for a sight-and-sound conversation than for them all to travel to the same place to meet up. It will be very much cheaper to call up a CD-ROM for a golf or tennis lesson via video, graphics and speech than to drive down to the golf or tennis club and hire the pro. It will be very much less hassle—once we have fast Internet access and quicker communications links—to let a browser search around for the best deals on travel or cars or houses than to shop around assorted travel agents, car dealers or estate agents ourselves.

But of all the potential beneficiaries of robust, cheap, easy-to-use, ubiquitous electronic communications, there is no one who will benefit more than the nomad. For him it will spell liberation. That's because robust, ubiquitous communications will mean he will not need to carry around six-pound PCs containing discs storing tens of millions of bytes of operating system software and hundreds of millions of bytes of applications software and files, massively powerful microprocessors and all the peripheral functions like floppy disc dives, CD-ROM drives and card slots.

Instead of these monsters which we today call portable PCs, the nomad could have a slimline, cheap ($200–300) so-called 'network computer' (NC) or 'information appliance' that will draw its operating software, applications software and processing power from a computer via the Internet.

Pursuing this idea are a host of top technology companies such as Oracle (the world's second largest software company after Microsoft), IBM, Sun Microsystems, Apple, Sony and Netscape among others.

Giving the proposed network computer or information appliance its capabilities is a programming language called Java, written by Sun Microsystems, which can transfer applications software such as spreadsheets, word processing or games to the network computer to allow the user to work or play with them.

The attraction of the network computer idea is its simplicity. 'The PC is a ridiculous device—the idea is so complicated and expensive', says Larry Ellison, Chairman of Oracle, who initiated the idea.

Another attraction of the idea is that it releases people from having to keep upgrading their $1100–2000 PC to a new model every couple of years 'or risk having that sinking feeling they've fallen behind the times', as Lou Gerstner, Chairman of IBM, puts it in advocating the network computer concept.

Naturally the idea of the network computer does not appeal to everyone. 'It's a stupid idea', says Bill Gates, Chairman of Microsoft, which has much to lose if Elllison's idea takes off. 'People prefer the attributes of local control to those of a dumb terminal', says Andy Grove, President of Intel which also has much to lose. Intel and Microsoft take most of the profits from the 60 million unit a year PC market to which they supply the vast majority of the operating systems and microprocessors. Ellison's idea, if successful, could substantially affect their businesses.

Time and the market will tell whether the PC or the network computer is the way the portable computer market will go. The struggle demonstrates the open-endedness and unpredictability of the high-tech industry. Even a basic product—like the PC can have its future put in question.

However, both Microsoft and Intel have set up units to look at the NC idea. Intel has considered how to build NCs around its microprocessor range, and Microsoft has announced a similar concept to the PC called the 'Simply Interactive PC'.

Despite their pronouncements, no boss of a technology company can afford to write off a new idea. All bosses know that the company graveyard is full of those firms which have ignored change. Remember the Chairman of DEC's famous remark, 'There is no reason anyone would want a computer in their home'.

For the nomad, however, the fact that the world's technology companies are turning their minds to the NC idea is very encouraging. The nomad's prime requirement is clearly portability and that means a tool stripped of all non-essentials. Carrying 320 million bits of Windows 95 around with him is clearly not a high priority for most nomads—just as carrying around the Official Airlines Guide is not a priority for airline travellers.

When they want a particular part of Windows 95 or a particular flight time, most people would prefer to download them into a cheap, portable device. And that is the function of the NC.

Matching the portability of the NC is another new idea called the Handheld PC or H/PC for which Microsoft has developed a special cut-down version of Windows called Windows CE. A number of companies showed H/PCs at the Comdex computer show in autumn 1996—such as 'CASSIOPEIA' from Casio, 'Velo' from Philips and Mobile Gear from NEC—and they are gaining popularity.

One significance of the NC and H/PC concepts is that big companies believe in them, so must have confidence in the communications links that will make or break their viability. So pressure will be maintained on the communications industry to increase carrying capacity and reduce costs.

Robust, cheap, easy-to-use, ubiquitous communications links are the key to the NC concept working, just as they are the key to the Complete Nomadic Toolset.

THE MIGHTY MICRO

'The invention of the microprocessor democratised the computer'.

Dr Ted Hoff, inventor of the microprocessor

JUST over a quarter of a century ago the microprocessor was invented.

It happened almost by chance but it changed the way in which electronics products have been built ever since—perhaps forever.

The birth of the micro started as a routine deal between a Japanese calculator company and a two-month-old, 12-person-strong, American start-up company.

The Japanese calculator company, Busicom, had produced plans for all the electronics circuitry for a new calculator. The circuitry would need about twelve chips for it all to fit in. Busicom wanted the American company, Intel, to make the chips for it.

At the infant Intel, a recently recruited former assistant professor from Stanford University called Dr Ted Hoff thought: 'Hold on. This is too complicated'. Hoff thought it would be a lot simpler if most of the calculator's design were done by software—that is, by a series of written instructions instead of actual physical electronic circuitry.

These written instructions could then be brought into play—used, reused and stored—as and when required by a single controller chip.

This controller chip was the world's first microprocessor.

It became clear to Hoff and others at Intel that the controller chip could be used for practically any electronic product. Those characteristics that distinguished one electronic product from another—say an electronic shop till from a traffic light—could be written in the form of software instructions while the controller chips could remain the same. So the controller chip could control a calculator or an electric motor, a washing machine, a computer, or any other type of electronic product.

It sounds ridiculously simple but, up to then, the conventional way of making the electronic circuitry for products had been to design the whole thing as a big, purpose-built, electronic wiring circuit and then reproduce it as a series of chips.

Hoff's idea meant that all the things that made one product different from another could be written down in software code as a series of instructions, while a general purpose, mass-produced piece of hardware in the form of a controller chip decided how and when the instructions would be used—a bit like a conductor controlling his orchestra.

Like all the best ideas, its simplicity took the world by storm. Above all, it revolutionised manufacturing costs. It was, and still is, extremely costly to design and manufacture purpose-built chips for a product. In 1971 Busicom was intending to pay Intel $100,000 for its twelve chips.

That's because 'hardware' design, i.e. physically designing circuitry, is time-consuming, requiring many man-hours of expensive engineering time.

Furthermore, manufacturing a few custom chips for one product is very expensive, because of the high fixed overheads of chip manufacturing, compared to manufacturing standard chips in large volumes for a large number of different products.

So the microprocessor made it very much cheaper to make electronics products. Moreover, their cost would always be on a declining curve because of the Incredible Shrinking Transistor. As the transistors halve in size every couple of years, so does the size of the chip—and the size of the chip determines its manufacturing cost.

Thus the invention of the microprocessor meant that all products based on it would decline in cost by roughly 30% a year. Or, conversely, they would increase in capability by roughly 30% every year without costing any more.

So in one fell swoop, Hoff's invention revolutionised how electronics products would be built, guaranteed that they would get continually cheaper and made a fortune for Intel.

Twenty-five years after the invention of the microprocessor, Intel had $20 billion worth of annual sales and a market capitalisation of over $100 billion, making it one of the world's most valuable companies.

Intel, and most other chip companies, have ridden the microprocessor boom until now about $40 billion worth of micros are sold every year and rising. Moreover the performance of micros has soared beyond all recognition from Hoff's micro of 1971.

One reason for that is the Incredible Shrinking Transistor effect which means that more and more transistors can be squeezed onto one chip for the same cost—so adding to the capabilities of a single chip without increasing its cost.

Another reason for the soaring performance of microprocessors is that the speed at which they do their work is also constantly improving. One of the effects of the shrinking process is that when the width of a transistor is halved its speed doubles. Since transistors halve in size every three years, microprocessor speed should double every three years—but in fact the speed increases even faster because of additional 'architectural' improvements.

The term 'architectural improvements' includes design tweaks, new features and new ways of organising the placing of the transistors on the chip. When combined with the effects of the shrinking process, architectural improvements provide a sixfold increase in microprocessor speed every three years.

This increase in microprocessor speed is important because the performance of a microprocessor, as a chip whose purpose is to control instructions, is measured by the speed with which it can process an instruction.

So if it takes half a second to take an instruction from the software memory bank and despatch it to where it needs to be used—say an instruction to 'turn on printer' or 'take letter A from keyboard and display it on screen'—then the micro is said to be able to perform two instructions per second.

In fact Hoff's first micro, which first worked in 1971, could process 60,000 instructions per second. That sounds a lot until you think that today's microprocessors process up to 500 million instructions per second (abbreviated to MIPS in the chip business).

But that's not surprising when you think Hoff's micro had only 2,300 transistors on it whereas today's micros have up to five million transistors. And the increase in speed is not surprising when you consider that each of Hoff's transistors was ten millionths of a metre square, whereas each of the transistors in a modern micro is a quarter of millionth of a metre square.

So, at the current soaring rate of progress, the BIPS or GIPS micro (a billion instructions per second) is scheduled for the year 2000.

The most obvious manifestation of the microprocessor's phenomenal rate of improvement is demonstrated in every High Street, where shop windows display computers which double in performance every couple of years for the same price.

It is said that Hoff's invention was as important as Gutenberg's because Gutenberg's printing press gave the great mass of the population access to books—which had previously only been available to priests and nobles—while Hoff's microprocessor gave the people access to computing power which had previously only been affordable by companies and governments.

So microprocessors are the key element in the advance of electronics products. They are also a very competitive element with all the world's major microelectronics companies nowadays fighting to compete with each other by making better micros.

Each company tries to design a superior micro which performs better in terms of MIPS than competitors' micros. So squeezing more MIPS out of a chip is the name of the game. However, it is a complicated game and designing microprocessors is regarded as one of the most intellectually challenging tasks within the electronics industry.

For instance, the PowerPC microprocessor, jointly developed by IBM, Apple and Motorola, has a team of some 700 designers at its Texas design centre. Intel's microprocessor designers today number over 1,000.

That's why a chapter on microprocessors is necessary in a book about building the tools of nomadism. More than any other component used in electronics, the microprocessor is the one with the fastest increase in performance.

This is just as well because microprocessors for the Complete Nomadic Toolset—unlike micros in the past which have mainly had to handle only text, graphics and sound—will have to be able to process in addition video, 3D graphics, videoconferencing, wireless communications, TV, etc. ('multimedia' in the modern phraseology). These different media types all used to be analogue, and very different from each other; nowadays they are all digital, or becoming so.

However, although digitising every form of media means that one microprocessor can handle all of them—sound, video, graphics, photographs, speech, etc.—it also means that micro-processors have to work faster to cope with hugely escalating volumes of digital data.

For example, a printed page of text is equivalent to several kilobytes of digital data. If you put in a picture which has to be converted into digital data you increase the amount of digital data by a factor of about ten, to several tens of kilobytes.

When we come to the kind of moving picture data used for television, we have to be able to process a high-quality picture 30 times a second (that is the 'frame-rate' at which TV pictures are transmitted). So, when it comes to video or TV pictures, micros have to be capable of processing vast amounts of digital data very quickly indeed.

The second important factor is cost. If everyone, in the Nomadic Age, is to be able to communicate with everyone else, the necessary tools cannot be restricted to the office or workplace—they have to be made personal. Taking these tools out of the office and making them affordable as personal items requires a price revolution.

With the calculator, the TV set and the computer, the key to personalisation was cost, and there are other examples where a price revolution has changed a product almost overnight from being restricted solely to the office or workplace, to enjoying widespread use as a personal item.

What must be kept in mind, however, is the importance of maintaining, or even improving, performance when cutting prices.

With the need to process constantly increasing amounts of multimedia information at ever higher speeds, and to handle the enormous volumes of data required for high-definition, three-dimensional graphics, the demand for constantly improving microprocessor performance is increasing.

At the same time as performance is cranked up, price has to be forced down. The important thing is to improve performance per unit cost—in other words, to offer a dramatic increase in cost-performance.

The third major requirement is to reduce power consumption for the sake of portability. A computer that can be used anywhere, anytime, must be battery driven, and it must have acceptable battery life.

Many people have suffered the experience of having their note-book PC dying on them while travelling or in a hotel lobby or airport where they have no access to a power source. So reducing the power consumption of Nomadic Age portable information terminals is absolutely essential.

Looking back, calculators and watches also have a history of meeting technological challenges in order to achieve this kind of improved portability. The earliest electric calculators were plugged into a power outlet, but these days low-power, long-life portable models are the norm with many of the smaller ones using solar-powered batteries.

A striking recent example is the rapid growth in the use of GSM (Groupe Spéciale Mobile—the European digital wireless telephone system), PHS (Personal Handiphone System—the Japanese digital wireless telephone system), and other kinds of mobile phones.

While the driving forces behind the rapid popularisation of mobile phones are the construction of a communications infrastructure and lower handset prices, the improved portability offered by power-saving designs is also a major factor. Portability–power-saving design, in other words, has a major influence on the commercial value of mobile phones.

So three features emerge as requirements for portable information terminals in the Nomadic Age: higher performance, price revolution (personalisation), and low power consumption.

The history of semiconductors is unparalleled in exemplifying the continuing achievement of all three of the above requirements, and the role that has come to be fulfilled by microprocessors is particularly important.

Semiconductors, with their continual drastic innovations—and especially microprocessors, characterized by high performance, low price, and low power consumption—are expected to play a major role in making the nomadic society a reality.

Microprocessor processing performance has made dramatic progress thanks to the combined effects of advances in both architecture (i.e. the physical design and structure of the chip and how the transistors are laid out on it) and the effect of the Incredible Shrinking Transistor.

The world's first microprocessor is an example of how the needs of users and the advance of technology can come together to create a totally new chip concept. This first microprocessor—Intel's chip known as the 4004—could process 4-bit data units (i.e. four 1s or four 0s or any combination thereof) with a single instruction; it operated at less than one hundredth the frequency (speed) of today's microprocessors, and delivered a performance which was one ten-thousandth of the performance of the latest microprocessors.

In 1971, the limit of semiconductor technology (i.e. the smallest width of the circuit lines and the diameter of the transistors) used in production was 10 millionths of a metre (10 microns) compared to a quarter of a micron on today's micros. The effect of that difference in manufacturing technology is that the 1971 chip contained 2,300 transistors while a 1997 micro has five million transistors.

In 1972, microprocessor performance was significantly enhanced by increasing the size of the data unit that could be processed by a single instruction from four to eight bits.

These early microprocessors were used in calculators, point-of-sale terminals, cash registers, and similar machines mainly used in offices. The microprocessor did not start to fulfil its destiny as something which would have a major effect on the lifestyle of ordinary people until, seven years after the birth of the micro, Apple used it to make its 1978 personal computer—to many people the most important invention of the 21st century.

Three years after Apple, IBM followed with the IBM-PC. It used a microprocessor designed by Intel called the 8088—an 8-bit microprocessor, with a performance level of around 500,000 instructions per second. The subsequent history of the personal computer is one of dramatic increases in performance.

Raising the performance of a microprocessor depends on two things: increasing the micro's speed (called the 'operating frequency') and finding new design techniques to improve the way in which the flow of instructions is processed (called 'architectural' improvements).

As the operating frequency increases, so does the processing capacity (i.e. the number of MIPS processed). However, it's possible to keep to the same basic operating frequency or speed while increasing the number of instructions processed per second by using new architectural techniques.

So, better performance is achieved through the combined effects of increasing the operating frequency and improving the architecture.

First, let's look at the question of increasing the basic operating frequency.

Operating frequency, also called 'clock frequency', is a measure of speed based on the number of operations a microprocessor can perform in one second.

For instance you might measure a knitter's performance by their 'stitch frequency'—the number of stitches they can knit in a second. If you decided to coin a name for a unit of stitch rate—let's call it a Bill—then you could say a knitting rate of one stitch per second is measured as one Bill. A prodigy capable of 10 stitches a second would be rated a 10 Bill knitter. It's the same with a microprocessor's operating frequency.

If a microprocessor has a 'clock speed' or 'operating frequency' which allows it to perform one operation per second, the microprocessor is rated at one hertz (abbreviated to 1 Hz), named after the 19th century German physicist Heinrich Hertz.

If a micro can perform 1,000 operations per second it is rated at 1,000 hertz (1 kilohertz or 1 kHz); if a million operations per second it is rated at one million hertz (1 Megahertz or 1 MHz).

Up to now, a microprocessor has usually needed one operation to process one instruction, so a micro with an operating frequency of 1 MHz can perform a million instructions per second (1 MIPS).

However, as we shall see later, some clever architectural advances have made it possible for some microprocessors (called 'super-scalar' microprocessors) to perform more than one instruction per operation (or per clock).

In the early 1980s, operating/clock frequency was around 5–10 MHz, but in the 1990s it has increased to 100–300 MHz. This trend can be expected to continue in the future.

What has made this increase in operating frequency possible is the Incredible Shrinking Transistor effect—whereby the speed of the transistor doubles every time its width is halved—and architectural improvements, of which some of the most important come under the general label of RISC (Reduced Instruction Set Computer) technology.

As its name suggests, a RISC microprocessor uses a small number of instructions compared to a traditional CISC (Complex Instruction Set Computer) type of microprocessor which uses a relatively large number of instructions.

CISC micros contain all the software instructions for general basic operation. But problems arose with CISC as more and more functions needed to be added to microprocessors and so more and more transistors were needed to handle them.

As the number of transistors on a chip increases, it becomes increasingly difficult to speed up the overall circuit operating frequency. The sheer amount of transistors acts as a 'drag' on overall speed.

If the operating frequency can't be speeded up, obviously the MIPS rate—the microprocessor's performance measurement—does not improve as much as expected. As in life, so in microprocessors, great size can mean a loss of agility.

However, the newly developed RISC microprocessors offer a solution to this problem. They do it by drastically cutting down the number of instructions used, so enabling the basic operating frequency to be increased.

The advent of the RISC-type microprocessor gave a big boost to the process of raising the basic operating frequency.

So the combination of the Incredible Shrinking Transistor and RISC architecture technology raised the microprocessor clock operating frequency at a single stroke, resulting in significant improvements in processing power.

For a time there was much discussion as to whether the traditional CISC architecture or the new RISC architecture should be the choice for future microprocessors.

The final outcome is that CISC architecture has incorporated the better features of RISC architecture, and vice versa, and that improvements continue to be made in the performance of both types. Technologically, the boundary between the two has become blurred.

As well as the Incredible Shrinking Transistor effect and RISC architecture, there are three factors which have greatly contributed to improved microprocessor performance: increasing bit size, 'pipeline processing' and 'superscalar processing'.

In 1971, a microprocessor's unit of computation (i.e. the amount of information which a single instruction could handle) was four bits (four binary digits). This doubled to eight bits within a year or two, then again to 16 bits in the 1980s. In the second half of the 1980s it further increased to 32 bits. Nowadays, 64-bit micros are on the market.

Because a single instruction became able to process larger chunks of information at a time, each instruction was obviously more effective—so improving the rate of throughput of digital data through the microprocessor and consequently upping performance.

In addition, 'pipeline processing' and 'superscalar processing' were developed as architectural techniques for improving processing speeds.

The first of these can be thought of as a kind of conveyor belt system. Let's consider a simple analogy from the world of cooking.

The process of cooking can be broken down into three steps: (A) cutting the ingredients into pieces of suitable size; (B) cooking them; and (C) placing the finished product on the serving platter.

The cook might carry out processes (A) through (C) for one dish before moving on to the second dish. But this approach is time-consuming. A more efficient approach is as follows: as soon as process (A), cutting, is finished for the first dish, this dish is transferred to process (B), cooking; then the second dish enters process (A), cutting.

Carrying out the various tasks successively, in this fashion, is the idea behind 'pipeline processing'. The number of pipeline steps normally ranges from just a few up to 10 or more. This method is particularly effective in increasing processing performance when operations can be broken down into a uniform number of processes.

The second technique, superscalar processing, is a kind of parallel operation method.

Instead of having only one processing circuit on the chip, a number are put on one chip, like having several microprocessors on the same chip. Obviously the benefit of this is that it allows a number of processes to be simultaneously carried out in parallel.

Thinking in terms of cooking again, this method is analogous to using several pans at the same time to prepare a number of dishes. With skilful scheduling, using a number of pans in this way is faster than using a single pan for successive cooking tasks. The key to achieving the benefits of superscalar processing is the skilful use of a number of processing circuits operating in parallel.

Although pipeline and superscalar processing entail complex processing and large-scale circuitry, they can offer major improvements in performance if used skilfully in conjunction with appropriate software techniques. These architectural techniques are consequently widely used in the latest microprocessors.

The process of reducing transistor size and improving architecture to increase speed is ongoing, as exemplified by RISC technology, pipelining and superscalar techniques. Another new technique known as VLIW (very long instruction word) technology is currently the focus of great attention as a performance-improving architectural technique.

The combination of architectural techniques and increased clock operating frequencies has produced some notable effects on overall microprocessor performance.

Performance has been improving by a factor of about 30 every ten years, and today, in 1996, we can find not only 100 MIPS processors, but some with a performance ranging from 200 to 400 MIPS. Based on this rate of progress, 1000 MIPS (or 1 GIPS) machines may be with us by the year 2000. GIPS stands for giga instructions per second, named after the metric prefix giga, i.e. 1,000 million.

What is important to note here is that this progress in microprocessors has been achieved with no significant cost increase. This has led to a dramatic improvement in the '$/MIPS' ratio, i.e. the amount of performance you get to the dollar—or 'more bangs for the buck' in the American industry jargon.

This improvement has become the force behind today's explosive growth in popularity of personal computers.

In the Nomadic Age, the demand for higher microprocessor performance and lower costs will become even greater, and the $/MIPS indicator will be all the more important.

To date, the $/MIPS figure has been improving by a factor of around 100 every ten years. When personal computers first appeared in the early 1980s, the $/MIPS figure was about 100. By the beginning of the 1990s a $/MIPS figure of 1 had been achieved—in other words, a cost-performance level of one MIPS per dollar. By the year 2000, supported by the demand of the Nomadic Age for a further improvement in cost-performance, we can expect to see a $/MIPS figure of 0.1—one MIPS per 10 cents.

It's all very well increasing the speed but the usual result of this is that power consumption shoots up. This is clearly unacceptable for the Nomadic Age which will necessarily be driven by battery power. Keeping power consumption to a minimum is absolutely vital.

In fact, despite the ever-increasing speeds achieved by microprocessors, their power consumption has been kept low.

Microprocessor power consumption is determined by three factors—the operating voltage, the operating frequency, and the power lost in the normal course of the electric current flowing around the circuitry of the chip.

The first of these factors, the operating voltage, is related to power consumption in such a way that power consumption varies in proportion to the square of the operating voltage. In other words, if the supply voltage drops by a third, power consumption will be halved. So, if 5 volts (V) operation can be changed to 3.3 V, the power consumption is reduced to a quarter.

Previously, an operating voltage of 5 V was the norm but, as transistors shrink, less voltage is needed to make them work, so the natural result of the Incredible Shrinking Transistor effect is that operating voltages have been falling.

As of 1996, an operating voltage of 3.3 V is becoming the norm for chips made on the mid-90s standard chip industry manufacturing process which makes transistor widths down to half a millionth of a metre (half a micron).

Since lowering the operating voltage has the effect of reducing power consumption, as mentioned earlier, 3.3 V operation is now the norm for battery-operated portable electronic products. This trend can be expected to continue, with a steady decrease in operating voltages to 2.5 V, 1.8 V and even 0.9 V.

Since a one-third decrease in the operating voltage halves the power consumption, the results of such decreases in operating voltage will clearly have a very great effect on reducing the power consumption, so making batteries either smaller and lighter or longer-lasting. This is a critical requirement for the Nomadic Age.

The second factor, the operating frequency, is proportional to the power consumption. In other words, power consumption increases in proportion to any increase in operating speed.

In view of this, variable-frequency operating techniques are being developed whereby the microprocessor is operated at full speed only when necessary, and at low speed at other times. With this method, the clock frequency of a 100 MHz microprocessor is dropped to 10 MHz when the microprocessor is idle.

An analogy with the fuel consumption of a car would be driving at full speed only when necessary, and cutting down on such wasteful practices as gunning the motor when stationary.

The third factor—the power lost through natural leakage as the current flows along the wires and through the transistors—is also proportional to the power consumption.

To explain from basics: the operation of a chip is achieved by turning its transistors on and off. Since the amount of power used to switch each transistor on and off increases in proportion to the amount of power lost in the circuitry while performing the switching, power consumption also rises proportionately.

The Incredible Shrinking Transistor effect has been a key factor in reducing the power lost through the circuitry and so achieving lower overall power consumption.

Also, obviously, the fewer transistors used, the less power is needed to switch them on and off. And one of the effects of RISC-type technology is to reduce the number of transistors needed to make the microprocessor.

So RISC microprocessors gain an advantage over the CISC kind in terms of needing to use less power to achieve the same performance.

An analogy is the comparative fuel consumption of a small four-cylinder car and a large eight-cylinder model.

Another way of reducing the power consumption in micros is by automatically switching off the bits that aren't being used. Obviously, in a microprocessor containing several million transistors, not all of the transistors are required to operate normally all the time. The proportion of transistors that must be operating at any one time is obviously limited by the purposes for which the microprocessor is being used.

So, by avoiding purposeless operation by unused parts of the micro, it is possible to reduce power consumption. It's a technique known to microprocessor designers as 'power management'. If we compare a chip to a house containing a large number of rooms, power management would mean turning off the lights and heaters or air conditioners in all unoccupied rooms.

Many techniques for reducing the power consumption of chips have been developed over the years, particularly for chips designed for portable applications like calculators and watches.

Many of these techniques were arrived at on the basis of a chip manufacturing process known as CMOS (complementary metal oxide semiconductor) technology. Originally developed especially for portable, low-power uses like watches, calculators and portable products, CMOS is now almost universally used to make microprocessors because of the overriding need to restrain power consumption.

However, while many such techniques have been used to reduce power consumption there have, at the same time, been dramatic increases in the scale of the circuitry, the number of transistors and the operating frequency of chips. All three increases cause higher power consumption. Clearly, increasing performance and decreasing power requirements are technologically contradictory requirements.

The success of the power saving techniques can be judged by the fact that despite increases in scale and speed, increases in power consumption have been kept in check.

The best way of measuring this is the MIPS/watt ratio—i.e. the number of MIPS you get relative to the number of watts you use. Over the last ten years the number of MIPS achieved to the watt has increased by a factor of ten or more.

In the Nomadic Age, the importance of the MIPS/watt ratio will grow dramatically, and we can expect to see a succession of breakthroughs in this area.

The contribution of RISC to the increase of performance of microprocessors can primarily be seen by the MIPS/watt ratio and the MIPS/$ ratio. These two ratios will continue to be the key performance indicators for future micros.

Another consideration for microprocessor designers is the issue of software compatibility.

As we saw with the story of the first micro, the hardware/software split is the secret to microprocessor design. It is vital to the successful operation of a micro to get the hardware working efficiently with the software. However, this is also very difficult to achieve, with the result that software gets written to fit the list of instructions (called the 'instruction set') compiled for a particular micro.

For instance, if Micro A has its own instruction set, which we will call Ai, and Micro B has its own instruction set Bi then, even if software performs exactly the same functions, software written for the Bi instruction set won't work on Micro A, and software written for the Ai instruction set won't work on Micro B.

Software written using instruction set Ai can only be run on microprocessor architecture A that has the same Ai instruction set, and cannot be run on microprocessor architecture B which has a different instruction set, Bi.

To make a human analogy, a book written in English can only be read by someone who understands English—no amount of expertise in French will help.

The effect of this is that software tends to accumulate around a successful microprocessor. All the software writers want their products to sell as widely as possible so they naturally want to write their products to run on the most successful micro.

As a result, a wide variety of software accumulates to run on a successful microprocessor. If software written for Micro A, using the Ai instruction set, is continually being developed and accumulated then the software resources built up in this way are a major asset of users, to be used and reused over a long period.

The concern this gives microprocessor designers when they are upgrading or improving their microprocessors is that they must make sure that all the existing software written for the Micro Ai instruction set can still be run on the new, improved version of Micro A.

For example, if instruction set Ai is improved, the new instruction set, Ai+, must be arranged so that the entire pre-improvement instruction set, Ai, is included, and the new portion is provided as an addition.

Subsequent improvements will be in the form Ai++, Ai+++, and so on. This is because the new microprocessor, A+, must be capable of correctly executing all existing AS software resources in the market.

This is the meaning of software compatibility, and shows why it is such a special feature of microprocessor architecture. If people buy a new computer with an improved microprocessor in it, they will be upset if it does not run all the software packages which they bought for their previous computers.

So, although other kinds of chips—say memory chips—can radically change every three years, when it comes to microprocessors, software compatibility has to be maintained over long periods of 10 years or more.

A typical example is Intel's personal computer microprocessors, which have maintained software compatibility from the early 16-bit era of the 1970s to the present 32-bit era.

Many existing users of personal computers have assembled a collection of various kinds of software, and it is only natural that provisions should be made to enable personal computer users to reuse these software resources.

While microprocessor software compatibility is basically a problem for a company's designers to solve, for the company's management software compatibility is vital to building a successful business selling microprocessors.

That's because, when a particular microprocessor architecture becomes widely used in the market, a large stock of software products using the instruction set for that architecture will be built up. If these software resources are to be reused, it will not be possible to use a microprocessor with a different architecture that does not offer software compatibility.

In other words, the existing microprocessor architecture cannot easily be replaced, because of the sheer volume of software that has been written specifically for it.

So, once a microprocessor architecture has come into widespread use, it secures an extremely advantageous monopolistic position in the market, unless a new one has distinct advantages.

In the world of microprocessor architecture, it is very difficult for a new architecture to displace one that preceded it onto the market.

Since a successful microprocessor architecture has enormous value, there is fierce competition to secure a monopolistic position in the market.

There are also frequent cases of cooperative ventures between manufacturers. This may result in a conflict of interests between manufacturers, and may also lead to various legal problems concerning the intellectual property rights to the architecture.

An example is the lengthy lawsuit between Intel and Advanced Micro Devices in the 1980s and 1990s (settled in 1995) which was fought over the rights to Intel's microprocessor architecture—the 'x86' architecture used in all Intel's microprocessors from the 8086 of 1976 to the Pentium Pro of 1996.

However, there is a penalty for maintaining software compatibility. It means that some of the new architectural advances cannot be incorporated in new versions of the micros so cannot increase their levels of performance as quickly as they could if software compatibility was not required.

In new application areas, on the other hand, there is little existing software, and software compatibility is comparatively unimportant

New application areas therefore provide an environment conducive to the development of new microprocessor architectures. So a good time to bring out a new microprocessor architecture is during the transition period from a dominant equipment-type to a new equipment-type.

Such a transition period is upon us now with the transition from static products like a PC which plugs into the electricity mains and rarely leaves its position on an office desk or in the home, to new equipment for the Nomadic Age which is portable and battery driven and where MIPS/$ and MIPS/watt are the driving considerations.

In this new nomadic world, dependent on batteries, there is a pressing need for drastic improvement in cost/MIPS and power/MIPS performance ratios.

The development of previous microprocessor architectures has been restricted by the need for compatibility with past software, which has meant that dramatic improvements in cost/MIPS and power/MIPS ratios have been difficult.

Now, with the transition from the old static equipment type to the new nomadic equipment type, there's a chance for RISC microprocessor architecture to fulfil its potential to improve the cost/MIPS and power/MIPS ratios without being constrained by any requirement for software compatibility.

For instance, in November 1996, the first examples of a new breed of nomadic PC called H/PCs (Handheld PCs) were unveiled at a Las Vegas trade show known as Comdex. Although these

HPCs all used the Windows operating system (an abridged version of Windows 95 called Windows 'CE') they did not all use the traditional PC microprocessor—the Intel CISC Pentium type of micro. Instead, out of the seven H/PCs shown at Comdex, five used the SH series of microprocessor, and the other two used microprocessors with the architecture of MIPS Computer Systems.

The SH series from Hitachi was already the largest-selling RISC processor before Comdex, but it had not been used in computers before. Until Comdex 1996, the largest use of SH was as the micro in the Sega Saturn games machine, and it was also used in digital cameras and in car navigation systems.

H/PCs show how new equipment types find new microprocessor architectures to build on, and they also show how the traditionally separate business worlds of consumer, communications and computers are blurring as the industry progresses towards realising the portable, compact tools of nomadism.

RISC architectures are one of the key enablers of nomadic tools such as H/PCs because of their rapidly increasing performance and rapidly decreasing power requirement and cost.

While utilising a cut-back, abridged set of instructions, RISC maximises the ability to process multimedia data streams, i.e. to handle different types of digital data such as video, audio, speech, text, graphics, etc.

Also, special techniques are used in the instruction set to provide more compact software. More compact software means that less memory storage space on the chip is needed, which means a smaller chip can be made, which means that the chip costs less—and therefore so does the product into which it is built.

The net result of using RISC architecture instead of CISC architecture has been to cut down chip size and increase both operating frequency and the MIPS count. The cost/MIPS figure has immediately improved by one fifth.

These innovations have been made possible by the fact that RISC architecture has abandoned the legacy and baggage of the past and has been created afresh to meet the demands of a new era.

So, although traditional microprocessor architectures have established a very strong position in the market, thanks to software compatibility, they must eventually find that the source of their past strength is a future weakness.

By limiting their architectural development in order to maintain software compatibility, the future competitiveness of existing micros is hobbled by their past. This is an example of the phenomenon whereby, at the transition between equipment types, the strength of past success becomes a weakness, and the lack of a past becomes a strength.

RISC architecture, based on the market needs of a multimedia, nomadic age, and honed by the latest semiconductor and architectural technologies, has achieved a revolutionary leap in cost/MIPS and MIPS/power consumption figures. As the Nomadic Age progresses, we can look forward to major new developments in this area.

Another trend in the way micros are evolving is that hardware is becoming absorbed by software. You might say this is just a resumption of Hoff's original concept for the first microprocessor—doing more of the work in software and keeping the hardware to a minimum.

The difference between a hardware function and a software function is readily understood if you visualise the calculator on your desk and a calculator on a personal computer screen. The calculator on your desk contains special chips for performing calculator processing. It is a hardware calculator. A personal computer, on the other hand, does not contain any special calculator chips. The calculator on a personal computer screen is implemented by having the microprocessor in the personal computer run a program that performs the functions of a calculator. This is a software calculator.

The same functions can thus be implemented either by hardware or by software. And software is able to respond quickly and flexibly to the need for specification modifications or revisions—a major advantage in terms of system flexibility.

The impact of cheap, powerful microprocessors such as those of the new RISC type is bringing about a quiet revolution in the structure of electronic systems. This revolution lies in the shift from hardware to software.

Let's consider the personal computer modem (modulator–demodulator) as a recent example. A modem is a kind of converter needed between a personal computer and a telephone line in order to send written messages down the telephone wires.

Data in a personal computer consists of the 0s and 1s of binary language. On a telephone line, this binary data is transmitted as different frequencies or as a changing signal.

A modem converts the 0s and 1s in the personal computer to an alternating signal with different frequencies or changes on the telephone line when transmitting data (modulation), and converts signals with different frequencies or changes to 1s and 0s when receiving data (demodulation). So a modem performs two-way signal conversion between the personal computer and the telephone line.

Modems have the functions required for facsimile transmission as well as personal computer communications, and are widely used either built into personal computers or as standalone devices. They are also built into facsimile machines. In these kinds of applications, special-purpose chips with signal modulation and demodulation modem functions are widely used.

On the other hand, we can imagine these signal modulation and demodulation functions being handled by software rather than as special hardware chips.

The tasks of performing a series of analogue to digital conversions of alternating signals into digital signals and, conversely, of converting the digital signals back into analogue alternating signals can be handled by software.

Modems actually have a variety of functions in addition to those for signal modulation and demodulation. This is because sending data via telephone lines involves a number of complex international conventions covering such things as transmission speed, transmission procedure and error processing, and modems must comply with these conventions. For this reason, special-purpose modem chips are structurally rather complex. However, conventions concerning procedures, error processing, and so on, can be handled easily by software using a microprocessor.

Another example is the compression and expansion of still or moving pictures. Image compression/expansion technology is of great importance in the world of multimedia. As the volumes of raw data are so enormous, it is extremely useful to be able to compress the data for storage or transmission.

The algorithms for image compression and expansion are generally implemented by special-purpose chips as hardware. In the fields of videophones, facsimile machines, CATV, etc., various optimal data compression/expansion algorithms are used, and special-purpose chips are used for this purpose.

In this case, too, as with modems, image compression and expansion functions can be implemented in software on a microprocessor rather than in hardware.

In parallel with the reduction in system costs, due to the use of fewer special-purpose chips, it is becoming easier to change a product's function simply by changing the software.

So cheap, powerful RISC micros should produce a steady shift from hardware to software in a wide range of fields including image and voice processing and communications control.

In products of the Nomadic Age, RISC processors will not only act as the central control for a product but will also replace special-purpose chips for the image, voice, and communication processing control.

RISC architectures therefore make possible the building of high-performance portable information devices that feature greatly reduced system costs, low power consumption, and adaptability to changing circumstances via software modification.

This is why RISC microprocessors are the basic building block of the products of the Nomadic Age. But what a building block! Every decade their performance has improved by 30 times, their cost/performance ratio has decreased by 100 times, and their power consumption has decreased by 10 times.

That's some building block and its effect on the products into which it is built will be similarly dramatic—making possible the tools of nomadism.

7

THE TOOLS OF NOMADISM

'The Iridium Personal Communications Network is to be a low-earth orbit satellite network consisting of 66 intercommunicating space vehicles in six polar orbits providing total global coverage'.
Motorola company publication, *1996*

A big proportion of the brains and budgets of the world's high-tech organisations is going into developing the tools of nomadism: tools such as electronic translating machines, electronic wallets, electronic position-finding devices, voice-operated computers, and 'Network Computers'.

At the same time, some of the bulkier features of high-tech products—like screens and keyboards—are being replaced by new ways of entering or displaying information which will lighten the nomad's load.

Instead of using glass and plastic screens, ways are being developed for projection displays and for 'intelligent paper'—a material which receives electronic transmissions and displays them.

Keyboards are already being replaced by voice commands or by light pen. In laboratories limited thought control of computers is being developed.

All these technological developments stimulate nomadism—removing the bulky features of high-tech goods and allowing the nomad to travel light.

These are some of the things that are already here, nearly here or will be here within the next ten years. They are not all new capabilities—but they are new to us as consumer-priced pocketable items.

Pricing depends on the shrinking transistor and the number of chips to which a product's electronics can be reduced. When a product can be made with just a single chip, it gets reduced to the price of a give-away item.

That happened early with calculators and watches—products whose electronics can be contained in a few thousand transistors. That's because one chip could hold a few thousand transistors as early as the 1970s, and it's why the Great Calculator Boom of the early 1970s went bust.

The price of a basic four-function (add, subtract, multiply, divide) calculator-on-a-chip dropped from $200 in 1969 when it needed six chips to $15 in 1975 when it needed only one chip. A one-chip product spells price meltdown.

Now that the industry is routinely churning out chips containing several million transistors, much more complicated products than calculators can be reduced to single chips. Mobile phones, scanners, organisers, pocket computers, answering phones, speech digitisers and position-finders are just a few of these products.

That's an enabler for the nomad who must have affordable, and above all, pocketable, tools.

Position-finders are going to be particularly useful to him and they have just hit consumer pricing levels in pocketable form. They are a major enabler for the nomad because a nomad is always on unfamiliar territory. On unfamiliar territory, most people feel vulnerable.

If you're in a car you are dependent on road signs and maps. Walking, you are dependent on a map and compass. On a boat or train you are dependent on what the captain or guard tells you.

All that is about to change, thanks to the Pentagon and the end of the Cold War. For some years now, the American constellation of navigational satellites, called Navstar, has been made available to civilian users.

In 1993, the last of 24 Navstar satellites needed to offer high accuracy positioning was launched. By having a constellation of 24 satellites, four should be above the horizon at any one time. That is enough to be able to get a 'fix'. In fact six to ten satellites are usually available for a fix but four will do.

According to GEC-Plessey, it has been found possible to achieve accuracy to within two to three metres using the Navstar system. The US company Magellan has already got the cost of a pocket position-finder down to $200.

That's a machine which will simply show a person's position by displaying the map reference coordinates on a small screen. Magellan says the cost of these machines has fallen by 30% a year for the last three years and expects to see them down to $100 by 1998. The company's aim is to produce position-finders for the mass consumer market.

The reason why the price has fallen and is getting even lower is the simple one that the product's electronics can be reduced to three or four chips and are heading towards reduction to one.

GEC-Plessey in the UK and Rockwell in the US are the leaders in driving the market for chip-sets which incorporate all the electronics for position-finders. They see the price for the chips—at around $45 in 1996—dropping into the $30s during 1997 and the $20s in 1998. By 2000, all the electronics for a position-finder should fit on a single chip costing less than $10. That means the cost of the end product in the High Street shop should be around $30.

So far, apart from mountaineers and hikers who carry a pocket device which displays the map coordinates of their position, the main use for position-finders has been in cars.

In 1996, position-finding systems started to appear in expensive European cars. They have been in cars in Japan for some years. A screen shows a road map of the area you're in and a cursor shows the location. As you drive along, the cursor moves along the road on the map.

If the position-finder is combined with a route-finding system, then the driver can be given directions. Either on the screen or by a spoken command, a warning of when a turn is coming up can be given to the driver.

The same sort of system will soon be available in a pocketable form. Making it possible are fewer chips, cheaper and lighter flat-screens and new ways of producing projected displays.

The nomad would load a city map into his position-finder via a 'smartcard', or a CD, or from a wireless link into the Internet. Then the positioning system would look for its 'fix'.

It currently takes position-finders about five or six minutes to get a fix. Having found it, the instrument's display shows a cursor—winking or flashing—to show the nomad where he is on the map. The nomad could then enter a destination and the machine would plot a route on the map—usually with a coloured or broken line—showing how to get to the destination. Once the position-finder has got its first fix, it takes only about 30 seconds to get subsequent fixes, so the journey can be plotted fairly continuously.

As well as for finding out where he is himself, the nomad can use this position-finding technology to find out where his belongings are.

People are finding that a very good use for position-finding technology, now that it is becoming cheap and compact, is to combine it with the technology for wireless telephones (which is also down to three or four chips) and implant it in anything valuable which moves and might get lost or stolen, like cars and boats.

Position-finding chip-sets, combined with wireless telephone chip-sets, are already being implanted in valuables. If these are lost or stolen, they automatically telephone their owner and transmit their position.

As the combination position-finder/wireless telephone technology gets less expensive, it can be put into many more things, such as laptop computers, cameras and mobile telephones—all items that are frequently lost or stolen.

So cheap, single-chip technologies will mean that the nomad will have no difficulty finding where he is, finding where he wants to go, and finding where his belongings are. In an age when airlines mislay luggage, that's a nice insurance device for the nomad and it could be as small as a credit card as the electronics gets reduced to two or three chips.

Some things, however, can't be reduced in size and one of the bulkiest objects the nomad will have to carry around is a screen on which to display all the information he's getting from his electronic tools. Screens are getting thinner and cheaper all the time but they're still rigid, inconvenient things to carry around.

The nice thing about reading from paper is that it can be folded into any shape to take account of space constraints (like a crowded bus or train), it's light, and you can read it anywhere.

With a screen, however, you have to balance it on your knee or find a flat surface to read it. You also have to get the light right and try to avoid annoying people by all the electronic beeps and keyboard noises which electronic machines make. And you can't read a screen in the bath!

So if large, rigid screens can be replaced, it would be a big boost for nomads. Fortunately there are some alternative ways of displaying information in the development pipeline.

One of these is to project information onto a wall; another is to project it in a small tube with an eyepiece at one end—like a child's kaleidoscope. That can give to the eye the appearance of seeing a big screen.

The kaleidoscope route has been taken by the US company Motorola, which has used light-emitting diodes—the same type of display you have in digital clocks—to develop a unit which has a volume of less than a cubic inch and a weight of 10 grams and drawing 70 milliwatts of power which, when put to the eye, can show what looks like a 14-inch screen containing 14 lines of 40 characters per line. It's a way to put a laptop computer in your pocket.

Another answer to the bulk of screens, as mentioned above, is to project displays. If you can view the information you want to see by projecting it onto a wall or any flat surface, you can do away with a built-in screen. How is it done without all the bulk of a conventional projector? One answer is to use semiconductor lasers which can be miniaturised.

The scientific breakthrough for this, achieved in 1995, was the development of blue lasers to add to red and green lasers, so giving the possibility of infinite varieties of colours.

Companies such as Daimler-Benz in Germany via its chip-making subsidiary Temic are developing such laser-based systems. They reckon they will first hit the market in 1998 with a product based on the technology and will have reduced it to consumer-level pricing by 2000.

Projection displays would be a very useful replacement for screens once they can be made small and cheap enough.

Another possibility is to beam an image's light directly into the eye itself, displaying it on the retina—so you'd see a kind of floating disembodied image superimposed on the real world. A US company in Seattle called MicroVision is working on this approach to displays and hopes to have a product out in 1998.

A fourth alternative to conventional screens is an emerging technology which could provide a roll-up screen. A UK company called Cambridge Display Technology, which is backed by private investors including the pop group Genesis, is working on a screen which could be rolled up after use like a home movie screen.

The company is developing light-emitting polymers (plastics) which could act as a screen to display information and could be rolled up when not in use. Other organisations engaged in similar developments include the Massachusetts Institute of Technology (MIT).

Plastic fold-up or roll-up displays are one of the key products for the electronics industry, simply because it's such a convenient technology.

It is well known how we're going to deliver documents or newspapers or magazines electronically, but not much use if we don't know how people are going to read them.

It is by no means clear whether people, who are used to reading their news, magazines or business documents on paper, will take kindly to the idea of carrying around a conventional glass and plastic screen to read.

We normally want to read papers in places where a conventional computer-type screen is inconvenient: on the beach, in the garden, in the bath, at breakfast, in planes, trains and waiting rooms.

However, if you can develop 'intelligent paper'—a paper-like material to which you can transmit the news or magazine articles or business information—then the nomad will be able to read his paper in the familiar way—on paper. When he's finished, the nomad can fold up his intelligent newspaper and put it aside for tomorrow's news to be transmitted to it. Or the evening news.

Another bulky item in the Complete Nomadic Toolset which the nomad would love to dump is the keyboard. One way of getting over that is to use a light-based pen—but that still needs a sizeable pad on which to write. A better way is speech-activated computers. These are already well understood and are being used by the disabled. Chip companies are already producing chip-sets which can add this capability to PCs.

Being able to open and close files by voice command and to input and extract data by a spoken command will allow the nomad to leave the keyboard at home.

Another tool the nomad's going to need is his portable translator. Translation machines exist but they need to be run on large computers and they are mainly used for performing written translations.

For instance Hitachi has such a system using a 50,000 word dictionary (occupying 14,000 bytes of storage) for translating patent applications from Japanese to English.

Primitive portable word translators already exist. These translate a limited vocabulary of pre-determined words, phrases or sentences keyed in by the user from one language to another and display the translation on a screen.

What the nomad wants, however, is a portable, affordable tool which will listen to a person talking in a foreign language and instantly replay the speech in the listener's language. This is a product which combines a lot of difficult technologies—

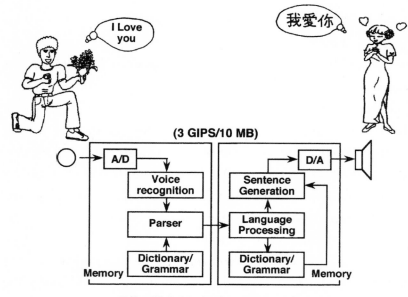

D/A = Digital to Analogue conversion

Portable Translator

recognising speech, capturing it as a digital text file, translating it, and replaying a digitised text file in spoken form.

All the advanced countries have been working on speech recognition techniques to develop products such as voice input typewriters, which will print out what is spoken. The technology is just becoming practicable.

Already voice organisers which can understand speech and turn it into a digital file are on the market for high-end consumer prices.

However, the personal translator not only has to recognise speech, but to perform the translation and speak it out again. This will require formidable amounts of processing power. It will require, we think, some 3,000 MIPS or 3 GIPS of processing power. At \$25 per 250 MIPS in the early 21st century, which is the expected cost, 3 GIPS of computing power will cost about \$300. Adding on another \$100 for memory chips and control chips, we get a total chip cost of \$400 in the early 21st century.

If we are allowed the assumption that, by then, the chip cost in the translator will be one-third of the final product price, then we could produce the portable translator for \$1200 to \$1500, or for \$1000 in high-volume production.

Some very chip-intensive products such as mobile phones already have a product cost only three times that of the chip cost, and a \$1200 to \$1500 translator would be approaching consumer affordability. And if not buyable, it would be such a useful nomadic tool that travellers would rent one.

So we can expect our nomad to be both navigationally and linguistically enabled by technological advances over the next ten years. The next important capability is financial. Here the electronic wallet comes in.

For most of his bills the nomad will use his credit card. Credit cards take care of hotels, car hire, meals, etc., but not small purchases—newspapers, cups of coffee, a beer. For these sorts of purchases a new form of electronic payment called the 'electronic purse' or 'electronic wallet' has been developed. The system saw its first practical trial in 1995 in Swindon, UK.

Visa and Mastercard combined forces with a common standard cash card system in the USA in trials begun in 1996 in the Upper West Side of New York City. It is designed to handle all payments under $20. Involved with Mastercard and Visa in the New York trial are Chase Manhattan Bank and Citicorp.

Before the New York trial, Mastercard and Visa had been developing different systems. That would have meant shopkeepers having to have two terminals for two different cards. Now it looks as though the two giants of the credit card business are sufficiently convinced of the viability of the electronic purse that they are going to standardise on one type of card and one type of terminal.

It could be a much bigger business than the credit card business. Mastercard estimates that over 70% of all US transactions worth $5 or more, and over 50% of the value of *all* the financial transactions in America, are currently implemented by using cash.

The electronic wallet used in the New York trials looks just like a credit card but, instead of having a magnetic stripe on it, it has a chip embedded in it. The chip—made by Hitachi—contains a microprocessor with a special memory chip incorporated into it.

The Mondex system trialled in Swindon is backed by NatWest Bank, Midland Bank (part of the Hong Kong and Shanghai Bank) and British Telecom. In 1996, Mastercard bought 51% of Mondex.

In the Mondex system, shopkeepers have a terminal incorporating a 'reader' which scans the card and downloads money from it in exchange for goods. The nomad can have his 'purse' topped up by phoning his bank and 'downloading' electronic 'cash' into the card's chip memory. (In New York he can get his money topped up through street cash dispensers.) The balance on the card can be spent in any currency the shopkeeper wants to charge with the terminal automatically making the calculation.

Plans for other Mondex schemes are being drawn up in Hong Kong, Canada and San Francisco. Visa introduced a different form of electronic purse at the 1996 Olympic Games in Atlanta, USA.

By 2000, the electronic purse should be well understood and widely used in the developed world. The value of the electronic wallet is that eventually it could replace folding money. Not only is folding money becoming increasingly easy to forge, but banks find that the expense of moving it around represents up to 40% of their total costs.

For the nomad, the electronic wallet means always having the means to pay for small purchases without having to go to Bureaux de Change for expensive currency exchanges.

The electronic wallet is just one of a number of 'smartcards'—credit cards with chips in—which will make life easier for the nomad.

One of the most familiar examples is the telephone card which is used all over Europe. However, smartcards are increasingly being used for many more functions such as getting into or starting a car, activating a mobile phone, giving computer access, allowing access to buildings and giving health information.

Brazil has a combined national insurance, tax and personal ID smartcard, Mexico has its 'tortilla' welfare smartcard and, since January 1997, Germany has its financial smartcard project covering 40 million people.

In 1996, Toshiba and Visa announced a consortium of over 20 companies, including Daiei Group and Netscape, to develop a smartcard project, starting in 1997, for all electronic commerce. They call it 'Smart Commerce Japan'.

As for credit cards, Mastercard and Visa are expected to switch over to chip-based smartcards from the current magnetic stripe type of card, by the end of the century. Other projects for smart-cards include using them for passports and driving licences.

This is all very helpful to the nomad because cards are easy to carry around, but there's a snag—the value of these cards makes the nomad vulnerable to muggers. To prevent this, a range of ingenious safety mechanisms are being developed to ensure that the possessor of a smartcard is its rightful owner.

For instance, the British Technology Group is currently running a 'Veincheck' project that looks at the vein patterns on the back of a hand. Vein patterns are as individual as fingerprints and can be scanned and compared to verify ID. This could be a commercial technology in 1998.

Fingerprints are a time-honoured way of verifying identity. In 1996 an American company called Advanced Precision Technology brought out a low-cost ($600) system for verifying Mondex cardholders by their fingerprints. The system captures the image of a fingerprint and stores it as a hologram. The card owner has a hologram of his own fingerprint included in the card. Any user whose fingerprint does not match up is rejected.

Other developers of fingerprint ID checking systems are Cambridge Neurodynamics, SEPT and VLSI Vision. Some of these are also involved in researching palm print recognition systems. Palm print checking is a convenient method for the cardholder.

Face recognition is also a convenient ID technology for the user but, presumably, faces can be disguised. University research into face recognition techniques is taking place at the Universities of York, Aberdeen and Essex.

The most accurate system for proving ID is said to be based on scanning the eye's retina or iris. Two companies researching the method are called EyeDentify and IrisScan. Although accurate, it seems highly inconvenient to users.

Voice recognition is yet another method of checking ID. There are a number of companies currently researching the possibilities: Gemplus, Vocalis and Domain Dynamics.

The European Union is funding a research project called CAVE (Caller Verification for banking and telecommunications) which is developing voice recognition for use in banking.

If on-line banking is the future of banking—and the banks believe that it is—then banks will have to find some way of verifying that the voice on the end of the telephone is indeed that of its customer. Voice verification is one of the key technologies for enabling on-line banking.

The voice verification technology is being developed by the Universities of Edinburgh (UK) and Aalborg (Denmark), by Brite voice control systems and by Agora Conseil of France. Trials started in 1996.

The ultimate ID method—which is being worked on quite seriously—is to detect people by their smell. There are sophisticated mechanical sniffing systems around from companies like AromaScan which can distinguish between different wines.

However, the thought of having to be sniffed by a machine in a High Street is likely to be more than most people will tolerate!

All these methods of checking identity by using personal characteristics come under a generic term in use in the industry called 'biometrics'.

Apart from biometrics, another important enabling technology for using smartcards for commerce is encoding ('encrypting') messages to make them secure. This is being worked on by companies too numerous to mention across the globe.

All these technologies—smartcards, biometrics, encryption—are working towards one end. They are aimed at allowing us to transact business with anyone in the world, wherever they are and from wherever we happen to be. They are creating and enabling the new breed of Commercial Nomad.

With the best brains in high-tech, and the largest high-tech companies, working together to empower the Commercial Nomad, his future looks assured. Consequently, the commute, the rush hour and the suburban lifestyle may all come under threat.

However, for many of us, the attractions of the nomadic lifestyle are not the opportunities it offers for commercial activities but the opportunities for leisure and pleasure.

For the Fun Nomad, looking for a cheap and cheerful way of using the entertainment and computing potential of the Internet, 1996 was a big year.

In February 1996 on a stage at the San Francisco Hilton Hotel, Larry Ellison, the Chairman and Chief Executive of the world's second biggest software company Oracle, demonstrated a prototype Network Computer (NC).

The idea of the NC is that it would be very cheap because it would not need a powerful microprocessor, a big internal memory, a hard disc, or any special features. Instead the NC would get what software it needs by downloading it off the Internet and would use remote mainframes for storage.

For Oracle it was a way of getting a few pennies in revenue every time someone downloaded a software package from one of its databases, or sent back a file for storage on an Oracle database. Those pennies were expected to add up—with 40 million users allegedly on-line.

Ellison predicted that sales of the NC would overtake sales of the PC by the year 2000. That takes some doing with a 1996 unit market of 60 million PCs.

Naturally Bill Gates of Microsoft and Andy Grove of Intel—the two people mainly responsible for driving the technological direction of PC business—publicly scoffed at the idea of the NC. But that did not stop Intel from setting up a unit to consider how such a device could be built around its microprocessors.

Two months later, in April in Amsterdam, Ellison showed off two more models of the NC as well as the San Francisco model. The latter was made to use a TV as a screen. Ellison also showed a laptop model with its own screen and a storage card on which to store whatever is needed while you're on the move. The third NC Ellison showed in Amsterdam was a wireless telephone-based NC with a small fold-down screen for writing and receiving messages. This is intended primarily as a communications device rather than a computing device.

The variety of NCs is the strength of the NC concept. The NC can be anything anyone wants it to be so long as it can access the Internet and cost under $600.

To the PC maker it can be a sort of junior PC; to the telephone maker it can be a telephone with a bit of computing capability stuck on it; to the games machine manufacturer it can be a games machine that can download new games—or anything else—from a telephone line.

Even pager manufacturers see pagers as a potential NC platform with makers suggesting that a simple 'push-button' access to the Internet is what most people want. Such a device could be made for under $100.

The breadth of the NC concept means there are a lot of potential manufacturers of NCs. Oracle doesn't want to be one itself, but it is very keen that others should take up the idea and so enable millions of people to download and upload material from Oracle's databases, thereby generating lots of revenue.

Some Japanese consumer electronics companies have committed themselves to pursuing the NC concept. They needed a new consumer product in 1996 and saw the NC as a good potential runner.

All this is very good news for the nomad, even though the NC is not yet the answer to his prayers, because he would still need a telephone socket and a TV screen to make a top-of-the-range NC useful; a telephone socket is needed for the laptop version, and the telephone version NC would not be useful for working on or for entertainment or downloading large quantities of information.

However, the NC is good news for the nomad for two reasons: it gets electronics companies around the world learning how to make combined communications/computing hardware cheaply; and, secondly, it gets companies developing the software links to enable hassle-free, quick access to whichever parts of the Internet a user needs.

Cheap hardware and easy access to information are two of the three key enablers for nomadism. The third is more carrying power in the communications links for the last few thousand yards to the home or the mobile phone.

As we've seen, enormous increases in capability are being installed on main trunk telecommunications routes with the fibre-optic cables. Capabilities of several millions of bits per second, even several tens of millions of bits, are possible.

But then the whole system grinds to a snail's pace (28,800 bits per second) for the last few thousand yards (called the 'local loop' in telecoms jargon) which makes the whole system inefficient for sending large amounts of data—particularly pictures. It is this constraint in carrying capacity ('bandwidth' to use the jargon) which makes the whole concept of the NC look impracticable in 1996.

In May 1996, the chief operating officer of Intel, Craig Barrett, pointed out: 'The industry should not be designing machines around the idea of unlimited telecommunications. The problem of bandwidth is getting worse. The pipes just aren't big enough'.

A 28,800 bit per second 'pipe' (telephone wire) isn't big enough to make the NC very useful. But one day the pipes will be big enough, certainly in the next ten years which is the time-span for the Complete Nomadic Toolset.

There is no technical problem. There are well-understood ways of widening the pipes for both wired and wireless communications.

There are chip-based solutions for wired communications such as ISDN which will increase carrying capacity to 144,000 bits per second and ADSL which will increase it to several million bits per second.

Then there are wireless solutions using microwaves which will also increase the carrying capacity of the local loop to several million bits per second.

Technology is not the problem. The technology to increase the bandwidth of the local loop is available here and now. The problem is the cost of installing it.

No one's yet figured out how to pay for the cost of installation of either a wired or wireless local loop. But they will. And when they do, the NC will enable nomadism.

All these enabling tools of nomadism—NCs, electronic translators, position-finders, electronic wallets—require an enabler of their own—batteries.

Take every kind of portable electronic equipment, and especially mobile phones and laptops which eat a lot of juice, and you find that a good part of their weight is the weight of the battery.

Solar power is one way of dealing with the problem, and that technology is waiting in the wings. It is already good enough to power many calculators. In time it may power computers.

But for the time being we are stuck with batteries, and the technology of batteries is in a state of flux as the base technology moves from nickel-cadmium to lithium-ion.

The key criterion for measuring the usefulness of a battery, insofar as the nomad is concerned, is the amount of electricity it produces in relation to its weight.

Lithium-ion polymer batteries produce 2.75 times more energy for the same weight as a nickel-cadmium battery. They can be recharged up to 2,000 times. They have been developed in the UK by the Atomic Energy Authority and in the US by Valence Technologies. A key supplier of lithium-ion polymer batteries is Ultralife.

As well as its energy/weight properties, lithium-ion polymer batteries have the big advantage of polymers (plastics) that they are flexible and mouldable. So they can be fashioned in any form desired by a manufacturer who wants to take advantage of any free space inside his product.

Technology development is making lithium-ion polymer batteries thinner and thinner. Ultralife have made one which is 1 millimetre thick. The battery maker Yuasa have made polymer lithium batteries which are 0.2 mm thick—about twice the thickness of the average sheet of paper, but less than the thickness of the cover of a paperback book and very much less than the thickness of a credit card at 0.76 mm.

So batteries could be made in the form of a belt, an arm-band, a hat or a shoe sole, or woven into clothing—even embedded in the body—so providing a portable, ultra-convenient power-pack for the Complete Nomadic Toolset.

A quick recharge is another capability making lithium-ion polymer batteries attractive to the nomad. They can be recharged in an hour.

The other thing which is changing batteries is the 'smart' battery. This involves putting a chip in a battery to make it charge more effectively. The result is a smart battery that tells you when it wants to be recharged and manages the recharge efficiently, making sure it is fully recharged.

Lithium-ion and smart battery technology will deliver to the nomad an efficient holding technology to power his nomadic tools until solar power takes over.

So the brains and budgets of many organisations—companies, universities, research institutes and the like—are working on the products which will make the nomadic lifestyle sustainable.

Translators, position-finders, NCs and electronic wallets are well on the way to becoming cheap consumer items. And the bulk and weight of the batteries powering these devices are being continually cut back.

Also the things that make these products inconvenient and unwieldy to carry around—keyboards and screens—are being replaced by new technology solutions like voice operation, projected displays, and batteries incorporated into clothing.

It is unlikely that a global effort already so far advanced, so well funded and so highly focused will fail to deliver the tools of nomadism.

8

MERGER FRENZY

'Big Brother may yet have a positive role to play—
keeping Big Business at bay.'
Kenneth Neil Cukier, Wall Street Journal Europe's
Convergence Magazine, *Winter 1996*

INSIDE the boardrooms of the world's communications and
entertainment companies the digitisation of all forms of media
and communication has caused alarm and excitement.

The familiar worlds of the entertainment and communications
industries are suddenly not so familiar.

In the old world there were established divisions: there were the traditional broadcast TV companies; the satellite broadcast TV companies; the cable TV companies; the traditional telephone companies sending messages along wires; the wireless telephone companies; and the content providers such as news services, film-makers, sports broadcasters and video distributors.

Now, instead of long-observed barriers between companies providing different methods of delivering a TV programme or a telephone call, ubiquitous digitisation allows companies operating in one branch of the media or communications industry to compete with companies in any other branch.

In the digitised world all these companies realise they are going to be in the same business—the bit delivery business. Every TV and telephone company—whether cabled, wired, broadcast or wireless—has the prospect of being able to deliver bits to homes and companies as efficiently as any other company.

So the winds of competition blow stronger and colder for traditionalists, but favourably for the acquisitive and the opportunist.

Further alarming the traditionalists is the disappearance of national boundaries as a barrier against competition.

Traditionally all that a TV or telephone company needed to operate was a licence from a national government and the company would then take a share of a protected market within that country's borders.

Nowadays satellite TV or international cables deliver messages and programming to millions of people regardless of national boundaries.

Programmes from Hollywood are beamed all over the world from satellites. Messages on the Internet are accessible by anyone with access to a telephone line or, increasingly, to a wireless network.

With technology overreaching national boundaries, there is going to be less and less chance for companies to grow big and rich while operating within one country protected by a government licence from competition.

Suddenly, if you want to be a major player in entertainment or communications you need to be a global player.

Governments around the world—led by the USA and followed most closely by the UK—are actively seeking to encourage the globalisation of the media and to promote free global competition. The governments of the most advanced countries at least pay lip service to the concept and those leading the way have removed national monopolies in the telephone service and have licensed competitors in their countries.

The subsequent story has been one of a struggle between the industry and the government regulators. As governments seek to promote competition and more company diversity, the industry has sought mergers and alliances to maintain its power over consumers.

On the one side is the need for choice and affordability of programming for hundreds of millions of consumers; on the other side are the corporate power and profits of the world's great communications and entertainment companies.

This industry–government ding-dong over competition versus monopoly is one of the great ongoing worldwide power struggles of the late 1990s, and no doubt of the early 21st century. If Big Business wins it, then the power of governments over their citizens will be greatly diminished.

The story started in 1984, when the US government broke up the AT&T monopoly telephone service in America, forming seven regional US telephone operators—Nynex, BCS Communications, Pacific Telesis, Ameritech, US West, BellSouth and Bell Atlantic (collectively known as the 'Baby Bells'). AT&T held on to the long-distance service.

In the UK, the government took away British Telecom's monopoly and licensed a second network operator called Mercury (a subsidiary of Cable & Wireless) for wired communications plus a raft of cable companies to provide both TV and telephone services and a number of operators of wireless telephone networks.

The Japanese and German governments are moving towards ending the monopolies of NTT and Deutsche Telekom and both have been privatised with flotations on the Japanese and German stock exchanges.

No wonder the boardrooms of the traditional communications companies are alarmed. If you've been cocooned inside a monopoly for 100 years, it is alarming to see the representatives of hungry foreign companies knocking on your customers' doors offering lower prices to tempt them away from your network.

So the alarm of the traditionalist communications providers stems from a number of things: first, they've got to contend with digitisation giving new companies a chance to get into the telephone market; second, they've got the geographical ubiquity of technology removing the protection of national borders; and thirdly, they've got the world's governments cheering on the process of encouraging more competition.

The reason why the world's governments are encouraging the break-up of the traditional telephone monopolies and encouraging competition is that they seem to have collectively accepted the view that reductions in the cost of communications will be a spur to economic growth—and growth is something which all governments want.

If higher growth can be produced by lower communications costs, and if the best way to bring down the cost of communications is to encourage competition among the network operators, then more competition there will be—even at the expense of thousands of jobs as the traditional telephone companies downsize. British Telecom, for instance, shed some 70,000 jobs in three years after losing its monopoly.

It may be bad for the employees, but the open competition/ price cutting trend is obviously welcome for the customers—a liberation from decades of arbitrarily overpriced monopoly communications services.

For the bosses of the traditional communications companies it's an unwelcome end to over 100 years of a cosy, familiar, protected way of doing business.

For new companies coming into the communications business it looks like a wonderful opportunity to get a slice of one of the biggest commercial pies on the planet. Because, as the old monopoly telephone operators have become privatised, it has become evident just how big that pie is.

Privatisation obviously means a float on a stock market, which means that a monetary value has to be placed on the companies. Immediately companies like NTT of Japan, British Telecom, and Deutsche Telekom of Germany leap into the ranks of their countries' largest commercial companies.

For instance, in 1996 BT's stock market capital was worth $30 billion, making it one of the most valuable companies in Europe. The November 1996 float of shares in Deutsche Telekom on the German stock exchange—which was many times oversubscribed—is expected to be followed by 'The Gold Rush of the 90s', in the words of a US fund manager. This new Gold Rush consists of an expected spate of privatisations of former monopoly network operators expected to raise over $80 billion during the final years of the 1990s.

According to US stockbrokers Merrill Lynch, European telephone network operators will be looking to raise $41 billion in share sales during the 1990s; Asia will try to raise $27 billion and Latin America $2.6 billion.

Deutsche Telekom's initial share offering raised $12 billion. In further share offerings by privatised network operators from 1998, France Télécom aims to sell shares worth $5 billion, Italy's STET plans to raise $6 billion and Australia's Telstra may also try to raise $6 billion.

That's why there's alarm among the bosses of the TV companies at the prospect of competition from the traditional telephone companies with these huge resources at their disposal combined with an anxiety to expand their operations.

And that's why, in Europe, government regulators have sought to prevent the merging of entertainment and communications functions in the same company. The UK government banned BT from sending entertainment down its telephone network.

Similarly, in Germany in 1996, when Deutsche Telekom considered a merger with a content provider, the German government prevented the deal because Deutsche Telekom owns 80% of Germany's cable network and could have tied its customers to a single content provider.

In France the telecommunications minister, François Fillon, went public in 1996 about his fears that the opening of competition in telecommunications could 'reintroduce de facto monopolies'.

However, in the USA the TV companies have been vulnerable to the newly privatised companies. Even the Baby Bells have revenues of over $4 billion each and the TV people have been alarmed to find themselves in the firing line of these well-capitalised potential predators.

For instance in 1996, AT&T paid $137 million for 2.5% of Hughes Electronics' DirectTV digital satellite broadcasting operation (valuing it at $5.5 billion) and has the right to buy up to 30%. DirectTV with its partner US Satellite Broadcasting offers customers 175 TV channels for about $30 a month and had 1.3 million customers in 1996—a tenth of the customer base of the largest cable operators, but expected to grow faster.

Analysts estimate that the number of customers in the US for digital satellite broadcasting services topped 5 million in 1996 and will reach 16 million by the year 2000.

So there's alarm from both sides—alarm in the traditional telephone companies at the effects of competition in telephone network operating, and alarm in the traditional TV companies about competition from the communications companies.

In 1993 the Americans demonstrated just how marriageable are the entertainment and communications industries. That year one of the regional telephone network operators, US West (one of the 'Baby Bells' caused by the split-up of AT&T), said it was paying $2.5 billion to buy 25% of the entertainment giant Time-Warner— the second largest cable TV operator in the US.

The same year the second largest regional telephone operator in the US, Bell Atlantic, announced an intended merger with the then (but no longer) largest cable TV operator in the US, Tele-Communications Inc. or TCI. The combined company would have been worth over $30 billion.

For a while the US West/Time-Warner deal and the Bell Atlantic/TCI announcement caused mayhem in the boardrooms of American TV and communications companies. Were communications/entertainment company marriages vital to their future survival? If they did not move quickly would the supply of potential partners dry up? Had they already missed the boat?

There would probably have been an unseemly stampede for the corporate altar had it not been for an unexpected fly in the ointment.

Instead of looking like dream romances, these mergers began to be seen more as *liaisons dangéreuses* as governments started to take a dim view of them. The view was taken that such mergers were contrary to the intentions of government regulators. The regulators were not slow to let their feelings be known.

The concern of government regulators was that, if instead of competing to reduce communications costs, companies in different communications fields join up to create new monolithic groupings to provide, say, both telephone and TV services, then they could use their combined muscle to keep prices high.

So mergers between communications companies and entertainment companies were seen as in conflict with the government strategy of trying to promote more competition and lower prices.

In the face of US regulatory disapproval, and a due diligence process that made Bell Atlantic think twice about the financial terms, Bell Atlantic and TCI called off their merger.

That did not stop agglomerations of power. For instance, the US TV programme maker Viacom bought a 'food-chain' of media assets—Paramount Studios, Blockbuster Video, and publishers Simon and Schuster—and undertook a major financial linkup with the Baby Bell telephone company Nynex. That gives Viacom the power to make films and TV programmes—maybe based on its own book publications—and distribute them directly via Nynex's cables into people's homes.

Despite all the efforts of regulators, by the end of 1996 the three biggest cable TV operators in the US all had cross-ownership shareholdings in each other.

Early in 1996, US West announced it was paying $5.3 billion for the US cable operator Continental Cablevision. With the Time-Warner cable facility, that gave US West access to 16.3 million US cable subscribers—knocking TCI into second place in the cable TV business.

In 1996 TCI had 15 million cable TV subscribers. It is the larges operator of the Primestar TV satellite system which broadcasts TV channels to rural areas unsuitable for cable. The company is also a big shareholder in Turner Broadcasting and so, following the intended Time-Warner–Turner merger, becomes a large share-holder in the combined group.

Time-Warner is the second biggest US cable company and has a cross-shareholding deal in US West which has an internationa wireless telephone joint venture with AirTouch. TCI also has a movie studio, produces TV shows, is a major publisher, and is one of the world's biggest music producers.

With these links, TCI is one of the most powerful TV companies in the world and, in May 1996, it agreed with Rupert Murdoch's News Corporation to form an alliance to own and operate sports channels on a global basis.

Or take News Corp. The company owns a traditional land-based TV company (Fox Broadcasting), stakes in satellite TV com-panies in the US (ASkyB), Europe (BSkyB) and Asia (Star and JSkyB), newspapers around the globe, a film studio (Twentieth Century Fox) and book publishers.

In November 1996 the holder of 13.5% of News Corp's stock, the US telephone company MCI, decided to merge with BT and the proposed deal was soon under investigation by European regulators.

BT had already been in talks with News Corp about providing a telephone link between the BSkyB satellites and TV watchers to give a two-way link between the broadcaster and domestic TV users. That would allow for services like home shopping and banking, consumer polling, Internet access, programmes on demand, etc.

Meanwhile, MCI had a 50% share of ASkyB, allowing the possibility of control and similar two-way links on the ASkyB satellite and, in 1997, News Corp and MCI announced they were taking a half share of another US satellite broadcaster Echostar Communications.

No wonder the regulators sigh over such deals. In theory they could produce exactly that restriction of consumer choice and competition which it is the aim of governments to expand.

Because whoever provides the equipment which gives access to the TV programmes, or to the Internet or the phone service, controls prices. And one box—called a 'set-top box'—can provide the link in the home to the TV, the Internet and the phone services.

The set-top box provides TV viewers with about 200 channels of digital TV, plus Internet access, e-mail services and a raft of two-way services like home shopping and banking.

In the industry jargon this access is called the 'gateway' and like the operators of toll-gates and toll-bridges of ancient days, the controllers of access can charge whatever they like, depending on the urgency of those wanting access. This urgency could be very great when the providers of the gateway also own the exclusive rights to important sports and entertainment events—as News Corp already does.

From the gateway owners' point of view the situation represents a virtuous spiral—the more people who use their gateway and the higher the prices charged, the more money there is available to bid to acquire exclusive rights to the world's most popular sporting and entertainment events. And the more of those rights obtained, the more attractive that gateway becomes to new subscribers, and the less attractive becomes any alternative gateway.

As the choice of gateway diminishes, prices can be jacked up without any fear of losing customers. Moreover, when one gateway becomes particularly widely used, then other companies wanting to provide electronic services to the home—banks, shops, travel companies, estate agencies, educational establishments, video suppliers, etc.—will all want to be able to use that particular gateway in order to reach the widest possible customer base.

Again the gatekeeper will exact his toll from all the new service providers, and the dominant gateway provider will charge the most. A monopoly gateway provider will be able to charge extortionately. Gatekeeping—as in days gone by—will be extremely profitable.

Small wonder that the plan is to subsidise the price of the all-important piece of gateway equipment known as the set-top box. It is reckoned that the boxes would have to retail at $750 each to cover manufacturing costs. Operators are said to want to sell them for around $300. Consumer goods have to be priced right to have mass appeal: $300 is affordable by most people; $750 will put off the vast majority of people from buying.

Clearly, with gatekeeping so potentially lucrative, it is well worth subsidising the High Street sale price of set-top boxes—in the same way that the sale of mobile phones is subsidised by the wireless network operators.

But the government regulators aren't mugs. They will be seeking to avoid exclusive gateways by making sure that the set-top boxes aren't made in such a way as to exclude all other service providers.

The battle between the regulators and the aspiring gatekeepers will be an interesting theme of the late 1990s.

Extortionate gatekeeping is one threat following the seamless ownership of all the different communications media. Another threat could be the mixing of news and entertainment to promote programmes.

For instance, the owner of such a conglomerate could ensure that lots of stories about, say, alien life forms are printed in the conglomerate's newspapers or news broadcasts to coincide with the launch of a film about aliens made by the conglomerate's film studios.

Or the emerging ability to make a realistic digital image of a person could be used to create news or to manipulate a person's image.

For instance, in 1996 a project was started to make a film starring the kung-fu genius Bruce Lee. Lee has been dead for over a quarter of a century. The technique by which Lee could be resurrected for a movie is to electronically scan thousands of pictures of him into a computer to create a digital 'sculpture'. Information on Lee's mannerisms, gestures, body movements and voice is also digitised and stored in the computer. The technique is promised, by its developers, to deliver an apparently living representation of a dead actor in a new film. They say that the image is identical to real life (on film).

There has been, it is said, interest in the technique from living stars. Marlon Brando is said to have been scanned. Also showing interest, apparently, are heirs of dead actors wanting to revive flagging royalty streams.

But there are also dangers for actors. As the US actors' representative body, the Artists' Rights Foundation, warned: 'An actor's first assignment will also be his last—once his likeness has been scanned there will be no further work for him'.

The technique offers such tempting prospects as seeing Marilyn Monroe singing 'Material Girl' or watching Fred Astaire dancing with Madonna.

The potential of the technique for political purposes is obvious. For instance voters could be wooed by seeing a faked digital image of a politician performing some imaginary deed of derring-do.

Or the same sort of digital image could be used to make a politician seem to do or say something discreditable. Or after an election, videos of a successful candidate making promises could be doctored to suggest that something else was said.

Another threat of what is called the 'back channel', i.e. the link from a TV set back to the transmitter, is the knowledge of an individual consumer which this gives to the owner of the transmitter. If linked to Internet access, for instance, it will tell the transmitter about the consumer's e-mail contacts, hobby interests, entertainment preferences, spending patterns and much more. Such information would be of great value to companies selling consumer goods and services, or to governments wanting to keep tabs on their citizens.

When it comes to voters, the information gleaned from the back channel could be of enormous value to politicians. In fact it would be possible via the Internet to tailor an individual message for each voter. A dog-lover could be assured of a party leader's love for dogs; a millionaire is told of the party's dislike of taxes; the unemployed could be cajoled by promises of welfare.

With integrated communication and entertainment companies capable of offering such valuable information and services to governments, one wonders how severe government regulation will be to curb the urge of such companies to merge.

These will be some of the issues affecting government regulators and company bosses into the next century.

For the nomad, however, the urge to merge could have good consequences. That's because you should get a much more reliable nomadic support service if one company provides all the hardware and the software.

If one conglomerate provides the equipment by which customers access its communication facilities, its own entertainment programmes and its own news and information services, then at least that one piece of equipment is likely to be able to work effectively across all the media types. And if it doesn't, you'll know exactly who to take it back to for replacement or repair.

So a single conglomerate providing a seamless range of services and the equipment on which to run them could produce a more robust Complete Nomadic Toolset than a tool which has to deal with signals sent by many different organisations.

Certainly this is one argument that will be used by the communications and entertainment companies when they seek to persuade government regulators to allow them to accumulate all the media functions, i.e. the different communications methods and the programming, under one roof.

Combining ownership of the means of communication with ownership of the programming has been one of the strongest business trends in the communications and entertainment industries of the last ten years.

One of the first to exploit the trend was Ted Turner of the American TV company Turner Broadcasting which was merged in 1996 with Time-Warner.

Turner started in the communications business as a TV broadcaster, then moved strongly into cable and, in 1986, began buying software—in the shape of films—on a massive scale. In 1986 he bought MGM's film library. In 1991, he bought the library of animator Hanna-Barbera which owned The Flinstones and Huckleberry Hound series. Later Turner bought a couple of movie studios, Castle Rock Entertainment and New Line Cinema, which gave him, it is said, the biggest archive of feature films in the world—some 3,700.

When pumped out of his broadcast transmitters and sent along his cable lines the film library produced revenues on a scale that propelled Turner's companies to significant size—quite apart from his famous innovation of the 24-hour news service, CNN.

So, buying up existing software, as Turner did, is one way to acquire programming to marry with communications abilities.

Another way is to buy up the rights to events. For instance, News Corp has bought the rights to screen all the matches in the UK's top football league—and with 200 channels coming via set-top boxes it would have no difficulty in televising them simultaneously with a lot of spare capacity.

Yet another way of acquiring TV programming is to buy up the people who are being televised. For instance Ted Turner bought the baseball and basketball teams in his home city of Atlanta.

One of the strangest of all the alliances is General Magic which included such illustrious traditional companies as NTT of Japan, AT&T of the US, France Télécom, Matsushita, Toshiba, Sony, Motorola and Philips.

One of the things General Magic is working on is the software for the Complete Nomadic Toolset. The company has developed software to simplify the use of portable devices which combine computing, communications and entertainment. General Magic calls the software Magic Cap and its object is to make portable computing/communicating devices much more simple and obvious to use—'intuitive' in the industry jargon—than the current breed of computers.

The idea of Magic Cap is that instead of typing out a series of instructions or clicking on a series of icons, as you do to perform a function on a current computer, you will control a Magic Cap-based computer through the sort of pictures you get in computer games, such as street scenes, buildings, walking around rooms inside houses, etc.

So you might, for instance, have a little figure on-screen walking along a street with buildings saying 'arcade' or 'library' or 'My Co.' or 'Post Office' or even have a telephone booth. Or he might walk along a corridor in a house with doors opening off marked with different functions, e.g. 'office', 'games room', etc. By controlling the figure you'll send him into the building or door which represents the function you want to perform.

Direct the figure into the 'arcade' to find icons representing games to play; or into the 'library' to find subjects listed on which information can be called up; or into 'My Co' or 'office' to find computing functions; or into the Post Office to find fax facilities; or into the telephone booth for phone calls.

The idea behind Magic Cap has been to recreate the atmosphere and achievements of the 1970s Xerox Palo Alto Research Center (the famous 'Xerox PARC') which first developed, among other things, the icon-based Windows-style, mouse-type control of computers instead of having to type in a preset series of commands on a keyboard.

The same goal as PARC—to simplify the way in which computers are operated—was the main aim of General Magic. To achieve it, General Magic repeated the PARC formula of recruiting some of the most creative software talent in the industry and setting it loose to free-wheel its way to new solutions.

Sleeping arrangements come with the work cubicles, job titles include odd-ball descriptions such as 'Wizard', games and toys abound in the offices. The appearance may be childish anarchy but the intention is deadly serious—to harness the soaring power of computers to work for the mass consumer.

As well as Magic Cap, General Magic is also working on another product that could be useful to the nomad—an 'intelligent agent' which you can instruct to carry out search and locate tasks for you.

If you want to find the time of the next train to San Fernando, or the cheapest flight to Bali, or the best kangaroo steak in Sydney, with car rental, accommodation and sight-seeing options thrown in—ask the agent, and it will scour the World Wide Web for the answers and display them on your screen. The company calls the agent Telescript.

The ultimate potential of Telescript is that it could create a global electronic market for every type of product and service. And it will be available just as freely to the Bedouin of the Sahara as to the Tokyo banker. It could be a major enabler of nomadism.

Some of the companies backing General Magic have already used early versions of Magic Cap and Telescript in products. The partners also have the right to take the technology developed by General Magic and develop it in their own ways for their own products.

Meanwhile, General Magic is further refining Magic Cap and Telescript. They may become the new standards for the Nomadic Age. Certainly the partner companies have the collective clout to establish Magic Cap and Telescript as standards around the world.

But in technology it is unsafe to predict winners. All too often a new idea comes from nowhere to upset all the general expectations.

The General Magic alliance is significant for two reasons—it shows that so many powerful companies are thinking along the same lines, and it shows that they fully appreciate that they can't do it all by themselves.

That also applies to other parts of the communications jig-saw. For instance even AT&T, the part of the old US monopoly that retained the long-distance telephone business, felt it had to acquire, rather than develop, its own wireless telephone capability.

AT&T did that by buying a wireless network built by an entrepreneur called Craig McCaw for $12.6 billion. The strategy behind

AT&T–McCaw is simple: people with mobile phones could dial into AT&T's long-distance wired network—a seamless marriage of wired and wireless. $12.6 billion gives a clue as to the stakes in the wireless telephone game. They are enormous.

Digital wireless communications networks only got up and running in the US in 1997, but the money paid to get into the game in 1995 and 1996 was mind-boggling.

In 1995, the US government sold off licences to companies wanting to offer digital wireless telephone services for a collective $7.7 billion, and then, in 1996, sold off more licences to companies wanting to compete with the 1995 licensees, for another $9 billion plus. The companies which bid for the 1995 and 1996 rounds of licences still had to build their networks—at a cost estimated to be as much as the licence fees.

The digital wireless potential in the US has attracted some major non-US companies to take stakes in consortia bidding for licences to operate networks. They include Mitsubishi of Japan, Ericsson of Sweden, Nortel of Canada, Lucky Goldstar and Pohang Iron and Steel of Korea.

It is because these moves into digital wireless telephone networks are costing tens of billions of dollars—which can only be recouped from call charges—that there's a lot of pressure to get things going quickly.

Moreover the example of the US in raising quite so much money will not be lost on other governments. So it is a powerful incentive to governments in other countries to close down their old analogue networks and auction off licences for new digital networks.

The beauty for governments is that, for technical reasons, a number of digital channels can be used where there used to be only one analogue channel. So closing one analogue channel frees up potentially eight or so digital channels which can then be separately auctioned.

Governments are unlikely to resist the temptation to sell off fresh air for billions. That's why the prospects for worldwide digital wireless communications are pretty good.

Furthermore, the Iridium constellation of low-orbit satellites—a digital mobile phone system which seamlessly straddles the globe giving connectivity to even the remotest regions—plans to start its service in 1998. Other such systems are being discussed.

Digital wireless communications are an important part of the future worldwide network of communications, being the best way to produce wireless phone calls and videoconferencing, to allow people in different places to see and discuss the same documents, or to exchange digital data of all kinds without the need to be wired up to a telephone network.

However, although the European GSM system is the world's most popular system, adopted by over 60 countries, the Americans seem intent on following different systems to give their own equipment manufacturers an advantage in the market.

This is unhelpful to the globalisation of digital wireless communications but not disastrous. Mobile phone manufacturers can produce mobile phones which can operate on all different systems. They may cost a little more than single system phones but that hardly matters in the heavily subsidised mobile phone handset market.

So the shape of the digital communications world is becoming clear. Digital television and audio broadcasting began in the mid-1990s in the US and from 1997 in Europe. For instance, BSkyB's digital TV broadcasts, beginning in 1997 with around 200 channels, plan to move to 500 channels.

Digital wireless telephone services started in Europe and Japan in the mid-90s and in the US 1997. The move away from the old analogue broadcasting and wireless telephone services accelerates as governments realise the financial opportunities.

Cable TV networks are ubiquitous in urban areas in the US and becoming so in the advanced countries of the rest of the world.

Meanwhile the communications companies, the entertainment companies and the equipment manufacturers are all involved with each other—more or less incestuously—to take advantage of the expected explosion in market demand.

There is so much investment, brainpower and energy chasing the goal of ubiquitous digitisation that it must become a reality—and sooner rather than later.

With it will come electronic communication that will be as universal and as robust as the present-day fax—but a fax that is not just text but includes sounds, voices, photos and video.

That's when geographic ties get snapped and when people become free to roam while remaining invisibly connected to all the communications networks and entertainment channels, and to every friend, relative or business contact they might want to speak to.

That's when the realisation will dawn on people that they have a brand new option to consider: 'Am I a settler or a nomad?'.

NOMADIC WORLD

*'A Bushman—gay, gallant, mischievous,
unpredictable and, to the end, unrepentant
and defiant'.*
Sir Laurens van der Post, The Lost World of
the Kalahari, *1958*

WHAT will a nomadic world be like?

The technology to enable nomadism will inevitably evolve, bringing with it the nomadic opportunity.

Whether or not people will take the opportunity is another matter. But what if they do?

After 10,000 years of settled existence, predicting the effect of switching to nomadism as a mainstream lifestyle is largely guesswork. But some effects seem logical, such as declines in materialism and nationalism, diminishing power for governments, increasing power for corporations, improvements in human relations, an easing of urban pressures.

For instance, one of the differentiating characteristics between settlers and nomads is the nomad's disdain for possessions. The nomadic Bedouin see too many possessions as a curse. The more of them, the more they weigh you down.

It takes a substantial imaginative effort to see most modern people adopting such an attitude! We spend lifetimes paying off mortgages to acquire property, we routinely borrow at outrageous rates of interest to buy household appliances and furniture, some people find even the act of shopping for new possessions a pleasure in itself.

Adopting the attitude of the Bedouin would take quite a change of mind-set for many people in the modern age, but could it happen? In some ways, it is already happening. For instance, we are getting less obsessed with the ownership of cars.

Thirty years ago there was a car air-ferry service which was quite popular in the UK, that could fly you and your car to European destinations. Nowadays we don't find it necessary to fly with our cars in the aeroplane hold. We don't think twice about getting to a foreign destination and renting a car.

Twenty years ago a car was almost as much part of the family possessions as the family house and the family dog—washed, cherished, even adorned; now it can often be the possession of a company and lent to its driver as part of the perks of a job.

So, to one generation owning may seem very important while to the succeeding generation borrowing or renting can be acceptable.

Could we also change attitudes to housing? In many countries it is regarded as perfectly normal to rent one's housing for a lifetime—even though buying a house is not particularly expensive as, say, in France.

Even in countries where it is thought preferable to buy accommodation rather than rent it, people tend to move house several times during their lives, suggesting that emotional ties to a particular locality are less compelling than the demands of work.

And the demands of work are increasingly encouraging nomadism. Jobs, in the late 1990s, are becoming more 'project oriented' to fill the gaps created by early 90s company downsizings. In project-type employment, people move from one specialist project to another at company after company.

The 90s corporate fashion is for companies to cut back on permanent employment restricting it to key staff in the company's core activity and putting out the rest of the company functions—information technology, personnel functions, building management, cleaning, catering, etc.—to specialist project workers or consultants.

Project working makes for high temporary rates of pay followed by financial insecurity, in contrast to remaining for a lifetime at one company in secure employment with predictable pay patterns.

So the lifestyle of project workers diminishes the attractions of a 25-year mortgage and increases those of short-term rentals. Project working necessarily entails a nomadic lifestyle.

If this continues to be the employment trend in the early 21st century, then the numbers of nomadic project workers will proliferate.

That means the numbers of people renting temporary housing rather than buying somewhere 'to put their roots down' is going to increase. For these people, as for the Bedouin, an accumulation of possessions will be a curse.

Even for companies' permanent staff, the likelihood of foreign postings—as companies globalise—is increasing. Many families welcome a foreign assignment, especially if the local culture is sympathetic, the climate is acceptable, schooling is available and the living conditions are adequate. There are increasingly few places in the developed world where people cannot find such conditions.

So, whereas our grandfathers' kith and kin would huddle around the stack, often living in a single county—even a village— nowadays there is nothing unusual in family members working in half a dozen different countries. Planes, phones and e-mail nowadays make physical distance relatively unimportant.

But, if asked, we still think of ourselves as settlers. We like to believe that somewhere is 'home'. But what underlies our belief that we are fundamentally settlers? Where, for many of us, is home?

Is it the address on which the mortgage is paid for the time being? Or is it where our books/CDs/stamp collections are kept?

Or is it simply the place where we spend more time than anywhere else?

There's certainly something about the place we were born, or where we spent our childhood, that has a big claim on us to be called home. A country, a state, a county, a town or a village usually has a claim on our affections as 'home'.

But what of the children of the proliferating project workers? They'll take nationality from their parents but can they acquire a sense of 'home' when they may have lived in half a dozen different countries before they are teenagers?

These children could become the forerunners of a generation which has no sense of 'home'. Home for them could simply be Planet Earth—a platform for work and leisure without boundaries.

What will be their attitude to possessions? Will they want the largest house a mortgage can stretch to cover—like their grandparents? Will they want to fill the house with expensive new furniture or even more expensive antiques—like their grandfathers do? Will they think it important to impress the neighbours by buying a new car every two years?

Or will they, like the Bedouin, look on material possessions as an encumbrance on their mobile lifestyles?

If they take the Bedouin view then they solve one of the world's most intractable problems—burglary. In some cities burglary is endemic—you could almost call it an epidemic—and the police seem to have all but given up trying to catch burglars. If people no longer fill up their houses with expensive furniture and belongings, burglars won't bother burgling. It won't be worth it.

If this really does become the attitude of the new generation then it could have a profound effect on lifestyles. Once weaned off the treadmill of pursuing and funding the acquisition of more possessions, people might find happier ways of spending their energies—perhaps on spiritual pursuits or relationships.

Relationships could benefit enormously from the nomadic life-style. As settlers we often get locked into a closed circle of friends or we become unduly concerned with impressing—or trying not to be impressed by—our neighbours.

A nomadic lifestyle gives the opportunity for meeting vastly more people than a settled lifestyle. The relationships encountered on the nomadic trail may be much less concentrated than those with one's settled neighbours—but it can be more acceptable to us to receive comfort, confidence and support from a stranger than from an old acquaintance.

When troubled do you turn to your neighbour? To a friend? Or to someone you may never see again? Many of us prefer the stranger, not wishing to display our troubles before our friends and neighbours. The modern growth of the practice of 'counselling' is an example of how we can accept comfort from a stranger which we might be reluctant to accept from a friend.

Also people often feel more inclined to be open and friendly with people they are unlikely ever to meet again. There can be an instant camaraderie among travellers where there are no consequences if the relationship goes sour or becomes embarrassing, rather than with people who you expect to see again.

Nomadism is a way to leaven the sometimes intense relationships engendered by settled life—the feuds with neighbours, the flirtations that go wrong, the embarrassments of which people's physical proximity is a continual reminder.

So a nomadic lifestyle, bringing with it a reduction in materialism, increased disdain for possessions, and improved human relationships, could be a good thing for the citizens of the developed world.

Could the Bedouin attitude win out? It's not going to happen quickly, and it's not going to be all-pervasive, but it could be an important influence.

Between the Bedouin and the Digital Nomad, however, there will be significant differences: whereas the main facilitator to the Bedouin's nomadism is the camel, the main facilitator for the Digital Nomad is a credit card backed by a healthy bank balance. Nomadism will not, for a while yet, be an inexpensive lifestyle.

As well as reducing materialism, the rise of nomadism could dilute the power of nationalism. When people can work in dozens of countries in a lifetime and holiday in dozens more, will the consciousness of one's nationality stay as strong?

For many of us, probably most, we consciously or subconsciously set a great deal of store by our nationality. However, in the Nomadic Age it is possible that this will come to be replaced by different ties.

For instance, it is possible that, instead of giving their primary loyalty to their country, people will give it to their company, a work group, friends, a religion, or a hobby group.

It is even possible that the idea that you must give your primary loyalty to the country of your nationality will come to seem a bit old-fashioned—even faintly ridiculous.

There seems to be a certain trend in this direction already. Global sects like the Moons generate intense loyalties in their followers and spread across the globe to every nation. Some multinational religions also inculcate the most fanatical enthusiasms among their followers.

It is just possible that nomadism will revive tribalism—groups of people coming together for survival, self-interest, shared beliefs or some common purpose.

A tribe of Digital Nomads may not necessarily roam the world as a group but individual nomads will, via the connected networks, be able to access the support mechanisms of the group.

The new tribes may be work related—the obvious tribe is a company, but it could be based on a trade union or a profession. Other tribes could be formed around common sporting interests or cultural pursuits.

There seems to be a need in the human breast to belong to something—to identify with a group. But in the free-travelling, free-wheeling modern world this loyalty may come less and less to be founded on love of country.

If associations of people in the future are to be founded on common interest rather than nationality, then it may be more important to know their interest group than their nationality in the future.

Nowadays, a citizen's licence to travel—a passport—is issued by a government. In this way governments can decide who travels and who does not, and can monitor who is travelling and where.

If the tribe becomes more important than the country, however, it could be the tribe that issues the passport rather than the country.

Some world licensing body—say the UN—could recognise a tribe as being licensed to issue passports, just as countries get diplomatic recognition which allows them to issue passports to their citizens which are then recognised by other countries.

In return the tribe would have to act responsibly in deciding who should and who should not travel and report on travellers' movements if the licensing authority wants to know about them.

The proposition seems less fanciful when you look at governments' decreasing interest in monitoring people's movements. When you drive across Continental Europe it is rare to find customs officers, still less border guards, checking your passport between European Union countries such as France, Germany, Belgium, etc.

At European airports the guards may be there for internal flights but the inspection is usually of the most cursory nature. Internationally, the requirement for entry visas is being dropped by increasing numbers of countries.

As travelling populations increase, maybe governments will be less willing to foot the costs of monitoring travellers. The tribe might take over.

Of course passports could disappear altogether to be replaced by a smartcard allowing police to make personal checks—for solvency, criminality, affiliations, infectious diseases, etc.

Governments will still be concerned about smuggling—particularly of drugs—and the entry into their countries of undesirables such as criminals; but these may become matters for the international police rather than the concern of national governments.

The decline of the powers of national governments seems to be an inevitable consequence of nomadism. For that reason, govern ments have traditionally persecuted nomads and have tried to persuade them into settled lives. That's because nomadism eats at the heart of what governments are there to do—to tax and to control their citizens. When their citizens are free to roam at will to work in any country, to pay taxes in any country, then govern ments lose a lot of their power.

Already governments' freedom of choice has been curtailed by the financial constraints imposed by the globalisation of the finan cial markets.

If governments tax too lightly, or borrow too heavily, or put interest rates up too high, or provide welfare too generously, the international financial markets punish the country. The punish ments come in the shape of things like destabilisation of the cur rency and stock market collapses.

Sovereign governments may think they can ignore the finan cial community which imposes the punishments, but nowadays financial outlawry from the world financial community would impoverish a country's economy. That's because the capital mar kets are already nomadic—capital can flow around the world unfettered and at the touch of a button. If capital is nomadic then, in a capitalist society, static institutions are endangered species.

Take the collapse of the UK government's efforts to stay in the European ERM (Exchange Rate Mechanism). The UK government was pledged to maintain sterling at a fixed rate to the German Deutschmark. Keeping the pound fixed caused great problems to the UK. Unemployment rose, the numbers of personal and company bankruptcies soared.

Things got to the point where practically the only tool the UK government had for keeping the pound at its fixed rate was to keep buying pounds itself and to keep raising interest rates—to the severe disadvantage of industry and sterling mortgage holders.

Scenting blood, the international currency speculators led by George Soros sold billions of pounds 'short' (i.e. pounds he didn't have but promised to deliver). Soros knew that the price was fixed, under international obligation, but he calculated that the UK government would have to pull out of the ERM and float the pound—inevitably leading to its devaluation.

During the Soros assault, the UK government spent billions of its reserves buying pounds and, on the last day of its membership of the mechanism, substantially jacked up interest rates. British house owners were talking seriously of abandoning their homes and returning their house keys to their mortgage companies.

That evening the government floated the pound. The pound's value dived and Soros and his followers could buy the pounds they had contracted to deliver at a substantially lower rate than they had sold them for. The UK's finance minister at the time—Chancellor of the Exchequer Norman Lamont—went on TV to blame 'unprecedented capital flows' for the debacle.

The economic policy of a G7 government had come up against the will of the international capital markets and the markets had won. The image of the sovereignty of governments would never quite be the same again.

Having demonstrated comprehensively that governments no longer have control over the value of their own currency when international capital flows freely around the world, the financial markets may go on to make the currencies themselves an irrelevance.

While Europe argues about whether to have a single currency or not, the forces of international finance could make the decision irrelevant—by issuing their own currency.

For instance, both at home and abroad we use credit cards for a large proportion of our purchases. When travelling, credit card purchases can be made in any currency and then the statement shows the rate at which the foreign purchases are converted into the cardholder's national currency.

If, instead of converting each foreign currency into the cardholder's currency, the credit card company issued a notional unit—say a Mastercard unit or a Visa unit—against which the value of each national currency was calculated daily, then there would be created a world currency outside the control of national governments or central banks.

That it can happen is demonstrable. It has already happened when countries play fast and loose with the international financial markets. If a country doesn't play by the international rules its currency gets ignored—it becomes an irrelevance.

For instance, when Russia first embraced *perestroika* the value of the rouble was so untrustworthy that everyone visiting the country used US dollars. Russians themselves preferred dollars to roubles. It looked as if the dollar would take over. By the mid-90s, the Russian government had sufficiently stabilised matters to be able to insist, reasonably successfully, that its population stuck to roubles.

But the Russian situation shows that, faced with a choice between impoverishment through patriotic attachment to your national currency and solvency through using a stable international currency, most people won't be too patriotic.

Losing control over their borders and their currencies is one thing, but what governments like losing less is their power to tax.

Of course no one is yet suggesting that national governments won't be able to fix their levels of tax for the foreseeable future, but their increasingly nomadic citizens will be able to vote with their feet on whether they'll stay around to pay them.

If governments want substantial numbers of well-paid citizens so that they can tax them, then it will be up to governments to provide the right conditions to create a climate conducive to well-paid citizens willing to be taxed.

The best way to do that is to educate and train your people well and support the local industries which will employ them. The next best way is to attract big multinational companies to locate their factories in your country.

Already we see governments falling over themselves to induce international companies to set up factories in their countries. Some extraordinary levels of grants are paid—especially in the high-tech areas which are seen as having the brightest and longest future.

In order to attract a single high-tech factory, which might cost $2 billion and employ around 1,000 workers, European governments have deployed assistance packages said to amount to several hundreds of millions of dollars.

When, in 1995, the German engineering company Siemens announced it would build a microchip factory in the north of England, it was said that the financial incentives were worth over $300 million.

In 1996, when the Korean industrial companies Hyundai and Lucky Goldstar decided to build chip factories in Scotland and Wales respectively, the assistance packages were said to be substantially more generous than the Siemens package.

So governments have to make themselves attractive to industrial investment if they are to have citizens well-paid enough to be worth taxing.

But they must be careful not to tax too highly for fear of seeing their high taxpayers leaving for a better deal elsewhere. Just as we are already seeing governments competing with each other to attract industrial investment, we may see governments competing with each other for citizens.

So one of the effects of nomadism could be the relative decline in power of governments. Stepping into the power vacuum provided by the retreat could be, primarily, industrial companies.

The big international companies are the big providers of jobs, the big generators of tax income and the big investors in wealth-creating projects. If they invest in an area, other companies commonly follow, supplier companies come in their wake, local airports, restaurants, hotels, taxi companies, etc., boom and the community thrives. If the big companies de-invest, then so do other companies and their suppliers, cash stops flowing into local service industries and the community withers.

This big company power to create or deny affluence to an area is a power which governments increasingly fear, and to which they increasingly pander.

As with international capital, the power of international industry stems from the fact that it is nomadic. It can pay its taxes to whichever government it chooses. It can shop around for the best regulatory regimes (usually the least regulated) in which to operate.

Moreover, international industry can quickly change tack. It can move away from one place to a more congenial region. It has an ever-growing list of increasingly generous potential host countries to choose from.

For instance, in 1996 the Prime Minister of the Republic of Ireland, John Bruton, publicly complained about the nomadic propensities of some foreign companies. 'One Japanese company is worth three of any other kind—once here they don't leave. For others it's just an excuse to settle in the short term before moving on somewhere marginally cheaper', said Bruton, adding: 'That's socially and economically destructive'.

The Irish Republic has attracted its fair share of foreign investment—particularly from American companies—and has more experience than most of the ways of foreign investors. So Bruton must have felt stung to make so sharp and so public an attack.

It shows that companies are becoming aware of the power which the nomadic nature of modern industry allows them to wield. This must be unsettling to governments which have pursued an industrial policy of attracting foreign companies to invest in their countries rather than growing their local industries.

Suddenly the prosperity of whole regions within a country—even countries themselves—can be out of the control of the government. That will give companies some power to affect government policies.

The sheer size of the annual revenues of the larger companies dwarfs the value of the gross domestic product of all but the largest countries.

For instance, large international corporations such as IBM of the US or Hitachi of Japan have annual revenues comparable with the gross domestic product of medium-sized countries such as Austria, Portugal and Finland—around the $80 billion mark according to 1993 estimates.

When it comes to small countries such as Guatemala ($9 billion GDP), Albania ($3.8 billion), Somalia ($1 billion) or Cameroon ($331 million), the economic clout of governments looks puny compared to the corporate muscle of the multinationals.

So it may not be too fanciful to suggest that the nomadic nature of capital and industrial investment will serve to tilt the balance of economic power in the world away from national governments and towards multinational corporations.

As the big companies become the movers and shakers of the world we might see future wars between companies rather than governments.

Killing wars fought over territory and resources—the inevitable consequence of settled existences—could be on their way out after thousands of years. Some of mankind's worst excesses have derived from the territorial imperative and the greed for possessions. For millennia they have spawned mass slaughter.

In the Nomadic Age, wars could be between companies with the casualties measured in financial losses and redundancies rather than dead and wounded. When companies lose wars and financial losses mount, they commonly get taken over, with the usual consequence that the company which does the taking over fires large numbers of the staff of the company acquired. It is a softer option than the results of traditional killing wars between countries where the populations of the defeated nations were killed, raped or enslaved.

Killing wars used to be the most costly of all human undertakings but nowadays inter-company wars probably cost more than medium-sized killing wars. For instance, the troubles IBM went through in the early 90s were at one time losing it a billion dollars a quarter—probably less than it cost to fight the war in Bosnia.

So for the future historian, killing wars could be seen as the dinosaur wars and new wars will be fought over markets. The war aims will be market share and increases in revenues and profits; the weapons will be the capacity to develop technological superiority and to successfully deploy the best brainpower.

However, although international companies may become the most economically powerful organisations, there will be other groups of people who will become very influential as the result of nomadism.

That's because nomadism could become—as it was in the past—a spur to tribalism. With ubiquitous worldwide connectivity, the power of special interest groups, sects, etc., could be greatly increased because they'll be able to act in concert on a worldwide basis.

For instance, back in the early days of Ronald Reagan's presidency of the US he took on the US air traffic controllers in an industrial dispute which led to many losing their jobs. What would have happened if every air traffic controller in the world had decided to take simultaneous industrial action in support of the US controllers? That would be a nightmare, especially for the tens of thousands of passengers in the air at any one time!

With instantaneous global connectivity such groups of people could plan globally and, if they do, they could become very powerful.

Governments vary in their legislation regarding employees' rights, but a globally orchestrated industrial dispute could make individual governments' legislation meaningless.

Global struggles between labour and capital would require new regulatory mechanisms which we haven't yet even contemplated.

Many people, from George Orwell in his 1940s novel *Nineteen Eighty-four* to Ridley Scott in his Hollywood film *Bladerunner* and subsequently, have pointed out a different scenario—that governments could use technology to gain unprecedented control over their citizens merely by gaining information about them.

There is a real fear that this is going to become possible as the networks become more and more a part of our daily lives. That's because every time you do something electronically you leave a 'digital fingerprint'—a record of what you have done—which someone else can monitor and read.

Already we are leaving lots of digital fingerprints. All our economic transactions are already recorded somewhere—whenever we pay by credit card. Already, when we use a telephone, a record is kept somewhere of who we called (sometimes even of what we said!). If we pay at toll booths with a credit card our travelling is recorded. If we withdraw money out of an ATM that is recorded by our bank along with every cheque we issue or pay in.

So we are already leaving a lot of digital fingerprints around but, with the increasing use of the Internet, the opportunities to leave more will be substantially increased. Every Internet page that we access can be recorded. Every e-mail can be read. Every transaction can be monitored.

The digital nomad, relying extensively on worldwide electronic connectivity for the information he needs to work and play, will be leaving digital fingerprints all over the place. This will make the nomad's life an open book to a monitoring government. It will also give governments the potential to exert enormous power over its citizens.

There is a partial answer to this problem—encryption. But encryption has never been an unsurpassable barrier to the determined snooper. The fact of the matter is that a tyrannical government could use this technology to control us all.

But it would have to be a tyrannical world government. Allow an oasis of liberalism and it is surprising how empowered this technology can make a single individual.

Take, for instance, the Saudi Arabian dissident Mohammed al-Mas'ari who left Saudi Arabia, settled in Britain, and proceeded to bombard Saudi citizens with e-mails and faxes containing allegations about the repressive and undemocratic nature of the Saudi Arabian government.

When the British arms manufacturer Vickers became alarmed about potential damage being done by al-Mas'ari's activities to prospects of its trade with Saudi Arabia, the British Home Secretary Michael Howard concocted a scheme, in 1996, to send al-Mas'ari to the Dominican Republic which agreed to take him in return for a rather large aid package. Howard's scheme was scuppered by the British High Court which ruled that al-Mas'ari had the right to remain in Britain.

The story shows just how much mayhem one man with access to the global communications networks can cause. And that power will increase as the capacity of the networks and their ubiquity increases—so long as there are liberal governments around to permit it.

Of course George Soros was a famous example of how one man with access to the networks—in this case the network of the international capital market—could take on the economic power of an entire country and win. Soros forced the devaluation of the pound against the wish of the government of Britain and forced the UK to change a fundamental plank of its economic policy—membership of the European Exchange Rate Mechanism.

Another example of one man wielding enormous power through the financial dealing networks was Nick Leeson whose speculations led to the collapse of the 200-year-old London bank Barings and the 1995 takeover by the Dutch ING bank. Over many months, allegedly single-handedly, Leeson was able to deal in—and lose—$1.4 billion apparently without anyone but him knowing.

Another example of the power which networks can give to individuals was shown by the saga of the Intel Pentium flaw. Intel, a company with a 1996 capital worth of over $100 billion, had produced a chip with a flaw in it.

No one knew about it until a college mathematics teacher, Professor Nicely, put up a statement on the Internet describing the law. At first the trade press picked up on Professor Nicely's observation, then CNN, then every major newspaper.

Although Intel did not think that most applications warranted a change of chip, it bowed to the media furore and offered to replace every flawed chip—and took a write-off, in 1995, of $475 million to pay for it. 'It took a barrage of relentless criticism to make me realise that something had changed—and that we needed to adapt to the new environment', recalled Intel's president Dr Andrew Grove in his 1996 book *Only the Paranoid Survive*.

It was not a changed perception about the seriousness of the law that changed Grove's mind, but a realisation that the environment had changed. He realised that, in a connected world, even one of the world's most valuable companies had to give way to opinion. And that opinion could be the result of the observations of one man.

So the possession of power will be a quirky thing in the Nomadic Age. Companies may gain it at the expense of governments, but individuals with special knowledge and skills will also be able to wield unprecedented power.

One of the ways in which the adoption of nomadism should make a very positive contribution to modern life is that it should take the pressure off cities.

Ever since the Industrial Revolution cities have waxed, and sometimes waned, on the back of investment in factories leading to the establishment of centralised settled workforces requiring accommodation and services.

For many of these cities, nomadism cannot come quickly enough. The stress involved in living in them is evident in the all pervasive burglaries in many Western cities, and the alienation drug-dependence and casual violence of many city dwellers.

Unfortunately, those with problems in the cities are often the poorest and the nomadic life is not going to be affordable by them—for the time being. But, as the networks become cheaper travel costs decline further, and with living costs so relatively inexpensive in the less developed countries, the prospect of leaving the cities may become affordable even for the impoverished urbanites.

Nomadism may then provide the answer to one of the advanced countries' most intractable problems—its decaying cities and the social problems and despair they breed.

The nomadic lifestyle will certainly have many, very different advantages and disadvantages to the ones suggested here. After all, if happens, it will be the biggest change in lifestyle for 10,000 years.

The only role models we have are the surviving nomads—the Kalahari Bushmen, the Bedouin, the Masai, the Fulani, etc. The lead unhurried lives, unmaterialistic, independent of government in tune with nature, spiritual, tribal and communal.

But is their way of life shaped by circumstance or has it survived because it refused to bow to circumstance? It all depends who you listen to.

Take two observers of nomadic peoples: Sir Laurens van de Post, who spent many years living with Africa's nomadic Kalahari

San or Bushmen, and T. E. Lawrence who lived and fought with he Bedouin of Arabia in the First World War.

In his 1958 book *The Lost World of the Kalahari*, van der Post describes the Bushmen in idealistic terms: 'His paintings show him clearly to be illuminated with spirit. The lamp may have been antique but the oil is authentic and timeless and the flame was well and tenderly lit. His capacity for love shows up like a fire on a hill at night. He alone of all the races of Africa was so much of its earth and innermost being that he tried constantly to glorify it by adorning its stones and decorating its rocks with paintings. We other races went through Africa like locusts devouring and stripping the land for what we could get out of it. The Bushman was there solely because he belonged to it. Accordingly, he endeavoured in many ways to express this feeling of belonging, which is love, but the greatest of them was in the manner of his painting'.

Contrast that with Lawrence's view of the Arabian Bedouin in *The Seven Pillars of Wisdom* in 1926: 'The Bedu were odd people. Had the circumstances of their lives given them opportunity they would have been sheer sensualists. Their strength was the strength of men geographically beyond temptation; the poverty of Arabia made them simple, continent, enduring. If forced into civilized life they would have succumbed like any savage race to its diseases, meanness, luxury, cruelty, crooked dealings, artifice; and, like savages, they would have suffered them exaggeratedly for lack of inoculation'.

One suspects there can't be all that much difference between the essential nature of the nomads of Africa and those of Arabia,

and that the reason for the different views in these passage
derives from the differences in the eyes of the beholders.

Nomadism won't affect human nature—the most that it can do
is change human behaviour. By changing human circumstance
for the better, by removing some of the stresses and restrictions o
modern life and by giving people a sense of connecting and
belonging, the emergence of nomadism as a mainstream lifestyle
could have a beneficial effect on human behaviour.

Silicon Senses

*'In contemplating the next millenium we
should prepare ourselves for a society in which a
more intelligent life form than ourselves will exist'.
Dr Kevin Warwick, Professor of Cybernetics,
Reading University, 1997*

T HIS is the chapter that really strains credulity. The truth is that the Incredible Shrinking Transistor will eventually make it possible to replace the five senses and the brain with chips.

Awful prospect? Or liberation from the effects of ageing, disease and injury? You can take your pick. But that's the direction the technology is going in.

Already there has been some success in replicating the senses, while computers could be thought of as a limited kind of brain.

The ultimate Complete Nomadic Toolset could be a chip implanted in the body feeding all the information about where you are, and where you're going, directly into your brain. And transmitting your brain's instructions directly to the airline, the hotel or the taxi firm.

It may sound outlandish, but the technology of implanting chips in the body and connecting them up to the body's own electrical circuitry is becoming increasingly well understood.

Implanted pace-makers for controlling heartbeats—once thought to be a radical notion—are now regarded as routine. Millions of chips have been implanted in animals to identify them or track their movements.

In humans, implanted chips have been routinely and increasingly implanted in deaf patients as part of hospital operations to improve hearing.

But it is not only hearing; the other senses—taste, smell, sight and touch—are also at various stages of development in the form of silicon chips. The digital ear, nose, eye, tongue and finger are already with us in some shape or form. They may be crude compared to real ears, noses, eyes, tongues and fingers but the history of silicon shows just how far and how fast the technology gets refined and developed. It's only a matter of time.

Then, of course, there's also the brain. As yet we're nowhere near being able to replicate a human brain in silicon. However, a modern supercomputer can obviously do some things much better than a human brain can—like performing complicated calculations or accessing and sifting through vast amounts of information.

Even the most monumental supercomputer, however, still fails to do tasks which the human brain finds simple, like recognising a flower or an insect or a face. There's a good deal of work being done around the world aimed at trying to add such capabilities to computers.

These efforts are a long way off from success. But one day—when silicon senses are connected up to a silicon brain—we will make a machine which can do everything a human brain can do.

It is not really particularly surprising that we can already make machines which mimic the senses—after all we humans are electrical in nature. The signals which the nervous system carries from our skin, eyes, noses, tongues and ears telling the brain about sensations of touch, sight, smell, taste and sound are electrical signals.

You could compare the body to an electronic product where the microprocessor is the brain, the wiring is the nervous system, and the input/output devices like screen and keyboard are the senses.

For many years researchers have been developing ways of connecting up human nerves to electronic wires making a direct physical interface possible between the human nervous system and machines.

British Telecom's Martlesham Research Laboratories have been doing a lot of work on implanting chips in the body with the ultimate aim of creating telecommunications networks that feed directly into the brain. BT is working with hospitals in the UK, and with the Mayo Clinic in the US, on implant technology. One project is a memory chip designed to insert into the brain which, inside the lab, is dubbed the 'Soul Catcher'.

The chip is designed to attach to the optic nerve to store incoming images which can be downloaded and stored on a computer. The chip could then be implanted in someone else's memory, allowing recall of an image seen by another person's eyes. Or, having downloaded the images to a computer, they could then be transferred by wire or radio to chips inside other people's brains, allowing one person to see through another person's eyes as though from a TV camera.

BT is convinced that man–machine physical links and the development of artificial replacement organs are inevitable, and is currently working on developing an artificial pancreas.

The earliest manifestation of artificial organs will be ears, reckons BT, and they are no more than three years away from realisation.

BT predicts that other artificial organs will become available steadily over the next 40 years: artificial hearts by 2010, artificial lungs and kidneys by 2015, artificial brain cells by 2017, artificial brain implants (i.e. chips implanted in the brain) by 2025, artificial legs and eyes by 2030, and an artificial brain by 2035.

Artificial implants in the brain are one way of helping the brain to keep evolving and increasing its capabilities, reckons the head of research at BT's labs, Peter Cochrane.

With the power of computers increasing as fast as it does, it might be a good idea to boost human brainpower by implanting extra capacity in the brain. That could be one way for humans to keep the upper hand over computers which are destined—if the creations of Hollywood are to be believed—to overtake the capabilities of humans sometime in the 21st century.

Diagnostic devices are another field where implanted chips are expected to be useful. For instance, all the business of sending blood samples to a laboratory for testing could be averted by a product being developed by the US company Motorola which is implanted in the body and which senses and feeds back—via a radio link—the composition of the blood.

For people like diabetics who may need to have their blood tested regularly, the device could be useful. For Motorola it could be profitable—some 20% of Americans are diabetic, estimates the company.

Research institutes in America and the UK have developed implants which can deliver electrical currents to activate muscles where the nervous system has been so damaged that it can't deliver the electrical signals to get the muscles working.

At University College London a device was developed which was implanted in a paralysed accident victim's back in 1994. The device had six electrodes connected to nerve endings in the back which, when activated, stimulated paralysed leg muscles into working. By the middle of 1996, the patient's condition had improved sufficiently for her to be able to stand.

The Illinois Institute of Technology in Chicago has been working for nearly five years on the same problem of stimulating paralysed muscles. It has developed implants about twice the length of a rice grain which can deliver electrical signals which activate non-working muscles.

Merely stimulating a muscle has some intrinsic medical merit of itself, because it stops unused muscles from wasting away, and so prevents pressure sores from developing.

Actually getting to the point where implants can restore mobility to the disabled is 10 years' away from realisation, says the Illinois Institute, which is currently developing a voice-controlled communications system allowing a paralysed person to signal to the implant which muscle it wants to work.

Eventually, it is hoped that a headband will be used which will recognise the electrical signals generated by the brain and transmit them to the limbs, directly translating thoughts into limb movements.

The notion of recognising the electrical signals of the brain is one that has been around quite a time. Hospital electroencephalographs (EEGs) which monitor the electrical activity of the brain are in everyday use. However, it is one thing to monitor an electrical signal and quite another thing to interpret what it means.

Among research institutes around the world which are seeking to interpret brain signals are Fujitsu and Hokkaido University in Japan and, in America, the University of Illinois, the New York State Health Department, BioMagnetic Technologies Inc. of San Diego, IBVA Technologies of New York, and BioControl Systems of Palo Alto, California.

Researchers at these organisations have produced helmets made up of sensors that can pick up the electrical signals created by the brain and can identify the different signals emitted when people think of different vowel sounds and words.

Researchers can distinguish between the brain signals generated when people think of different letters or words. With a physical link from the helmet to a computer, people can think of words or letters which are then called up on the computer's screen.

An American medical magazine reports the case of a multiple sclerosis victim who had no body movement, limited eye movement but normal brain function. It says that after a few weeks of concentrated effort the patient was able to rewrite his Will using a thought-controlled computer made by BioControl Systems.

At the New York State Health Department's Wadsworth Center, 25 people have been trained to use their thoughts to control the horizontal and vertical movements of a cursor on a screen. IBVA Technologies (the acronym stands for Interactive Brainwave Visual Analyser) uses an EEG machine to pick up information from a headband round the brain attached to a receiver which transfers the information to a computer. A US university using the IBVA machine for research is the University of Pennsylvania.

The technology has even reached the consumer electronics world. In 1996, in the chain of Fry's electronics stores in the US, you could see a game being demonstrated where you were invited to put your finger in what looked like a metal finger stall and then control your descent down a slalom ski course—shown on the computer screen—by thinking 'left' to go left, or relaxing the mind to go right.

The game is marketed by a company called The Other 90% Technologies of San Raphael, California. It works on the same basis as a lie detector—that if you're thinking hard the electrical resistance of the skin goes down. If you relax the mind the resistance goes up. The finger stall measures this change in resistance and reacts accordingly.

The technology would, naturally, be a superb one for the nomad who above all needs the minimum of kit to carry around. If he can control the equipment he has to carry by thought alone, it will make life very much more convenient for him. Controlling a computer or a mobile phone would become as instinctive and effortless for the nomad as waving a hand or walking.

One of the areas where silicon senses really are having an immediate practical and commercial effect is in hearing. Thousands of people in the 1990s with damaged hearing nerves, resulting in deafness, had an operation to implant a chip in their heads. On the chip is a radio receiver, a transmitter and a microprocessor. The receiver picks up sound signals sent from an external microphone, the microprocessor converts the signals from the receiver into a form understandable by the brain, and the transmitter sends the converted signals along wires to electrodes implanted into the remnants of the damaged hearing nerves.

The electrical signals from the electrodes stimulate the hearing nerves to carry the signals into the brain and hearing is restored. It does not yet deliver perfect hearing, but the technology is improving all the time.

Another approach to silicon hearing is to replace the cochlea— part of the ear's hearing mechanism—with a silicon chip which can mimic the cochlea's function. This approach is being taken by London's Imperial College of Science, Technology and Medicine.

Silicon hearing is the most commercially advanced of the silicon senses but it is not the most refined. A silicon 'nose' has been made sensitive enough to determine the vineyard of origin of wines and the origin of olive oil. It has proved to be better at sniffing out truffles than French pigs!

The nose has been developed by the British company Aroma-scan, and it is co-developing it with Mitsubishi Electric of Japan which has licensed Aromascan's technology. Aromascan also works with the US Federal Grain Inspectorate on checking grain samples and with the leading food instrumentation supplier Foss Electric on checking the freshness of dairy products and meat.

The nose works by tracking the reactions of a polymer to the airborne molecules that constitute a smell. The polymer's electrical characteristics change in response to these molecules and these characteristics are then converted into digital form.

The nose's microprocessor compares the digitised characteristics of the effects of one smell on the polymer with those of a databank made up of the electrical characteristics caused by other smells, and then makes the decision as to which smell it is currently sniffing.

If the process could be reversed and if electrical changes in the polymer could be used to reconstitute the molecules of a smell, then a smell could be electronically transferred across the planet and recreated. Sitting in the lavender fields of Provence it would be possible to sniff the smells of Bombay or, more agreeably, vice versa.

Silicon vision is another of the senses which has had a lot of attention. That's probably because it is seen as having a lot of commercial applications from adding sight to robots to restoring the sight of blind people.

The University of California has created a single chip which mimics the activity of the retina. The chip, the size of a postage stamp, contains 500 tiny microprocessors. The idea is to use the chip to restore sight to people whose vision has been lost through disease.

Another project, known as the 'Retinal Implant Project', between the Harvard Medical School and the Massachusetts Institute of Technology takes a different approach to the problem. Instead of creating a very complex model of the working of the retina like the University of California, it takes an array of photoreceptors—devices which can take light and convert them into electrical signals—and places them directly on the retina. The user wears a pair of glasses on which are mounted cameras which send images to the photoreceptors. The photoreceptors then convert the images into electrical signals which are fed into the nervous system and so to the brain.

MIT's technology is said to be at least 10 years away from use on humans, though it has been used in rabbits, and researchers say that it is clear that the rabbits see something—though they do not know exactly what.

At the University of North Carolina, a prototype silicon artificial retina has been created which attaches directly to a damaged retina. The artificial retina is for cases where disease, like glaucoma, has destroyed the eye's natural photoreceptors in the retina but leaves the underlying ganglia and optic nerve unaffected.

The chip is ground so thin that it is transparent. It contains optically operated transistors which can take light from the outside world and convert it into electrical signals which are fed into the ganglia. The first human trials of the University of North Carolina's prototype retina began in 1997.

Most advanced of all these research institutes into artificial vision for humans is thought to be the US National Institutes of Health where an implant in a blind patient is said to have resulted in restoring some limited measure of sight described as a 'shadowy picture'.

Silicon vision is not just being developed for people. Motor vehicles and robots are the two biggest applications where artificial vision is useful. Here the vision, instead of being designed to fit the human eye, is achieved by straightforward TV cameras. There is no difficulty about making cameras. The difficulty with machine vision lies in interpreting what the camera sees, processing that information and making use of it.

By using standard commercial chip manufacturing techniques, cameras-on-a-chip can now be made which are rapidly becoming smaller and cheaper. Camera-on-a-chip specialist Vision of Edinburgh can make a complete video camera on a chip measuring 7 millimetres by 8 millimetres, needing only a lens to make up a working video camera. Such lenses cost upwards of £1 and such a chip can be made for a few pounds.

So cameras are cheap and will get cheaper. Now they are on the chip-makers' learning curve we can expect them to decline in cost by 30% a year. In 1996 Vision was making 100,000 cameras on a chip per month and planning to increase that to a million a month. Higher volumes will drive down the costs and video cameras should eventually become ubiquitous commodity items.

IMEC, the Belgian microelectronics research institute, is producing a camera-on-a-chip which can tell you when it's about to collide with something. The idea is to add an element of vision to cars, to warn a car driver of an impending collision. The 'time-to-crash' camera uses an imaging sensor plus a microprocessor. It was developed by an ESPRIT consortium comprising CSATA Technopolis of Italy, BRDI of France, Krypton and IMEC of Leuven, Belguim, and PARS of Frankfurt. The camera captures the image of the object the car is about to hit and the microprocessor calculates—from the changing size of the image—how long it will take before the collision. Combined with very cheap radar systems which are also being developed as anti-collision systems, the time-to-crash camera could prove an effective way of adding artificial sight to cars.

Cameras are not the problem. The problem is getting a machine to 'understand' what the camera shows and to draw conclusions from it.

At the Media Laboratory of the Massachusetts Institute of Technology, a group under Professor Alex Pentland has produced a system which can recognise one face out of a stored database of 2,000 faces with a percentage success rate in the 'high 90s'. Pentland's group is also working on recognition of human expressions—fear, smile, anger, surprise, etc.—and, based on 10 image sequences of the various expressions, has achieved a 98% successful recognition rate. The MIT system can also 'read' sign language and can recognise 40 words in sign language with a 99% success rate.

Artificial vision is probably the silicon sense on which most money is being spent in research, but artificial touch is having a lot of money spent on its development and manufacturing processes.

Artificial touch is not yet delivered by chips but by pressure sensors which are nowadays made by the same manufacturing processes as chips. These processes make possible the manu-facturing of 'micro-machines', machines so small that they can burrow along inside veins, with features that are too small for the eye to see. This means that large numbers of tiny, micro-machined pressure sensors can be used to deliver increasingly refined and precise artificial touch.

Artificial touch is mostly utilised in industrial robots where their capability ranges from an iron grip down to the ability to pick up an egg without breaking it.

Artificial touch is also being developed for use in the gloves and suits worn for Virtual Reality experiences. Here pressure sensors connected up to wires can reproduce sensations that were gener-ated elsewhere. These sensations could be electrically stored on a disc or a videotape and then be transferred to the wearer of a Virtual Reality suit plugged into the TV, VCR or computer. Or two people wearing such suits could link them up to the public com-munications networks and swap the sensations of touching each other while on opposite sides of the planet.

A kiss transmitter would be a nice gismo for nomadic partners separated by travel. If these signals were to be digitised, then a databank of touches could be built up and used on demand. People expect the main applications to come from 'feely' videos—where feelings of touch accompany the images.

Of course the prospects of marrying implanted chip tech-nology to Virtual Reality experiences is awesome, or horrible, depending on your viewpoint. With chips implanted in the brain it would be possible to send these experiences direct to the receiver's brain. The prospect would then loom of people finding it quite impossible to tell the difference between real experience and artificially generated experience. That's one of the Hollywood-style visions of future hell if dictators control that technology.

There are obvious commercial reasons why people should put a lot of money into developing the processes to deliver artificial touch. This probably means that touch will become a fairly refined artificial sense in the medium-term future.

Taste, however, seems to be the poor relation of the artificial senses. No one has yet developed a tasting machine, though many have tried. As Aromascan point out, the ideal machine for the food industry—wanting quick mechanical checks on the freshness and taste of food—would be a combined smell and taste machine. But no one has come up with a commercial device.

However, the Department of Food Science and Technology at Cornell University in the USA developed a tasting machine as part of a PhD project by one of its students, Deborah Roberts. Cornell's mouth behaves like any other mouth—chewing, warming, salivating, etc.—and claims to be able to differentiate between the tastes of fresh raspberries, heated raspberries, and raspberries and cream. But as its name—'The Retronasal Aroma Simulator'—suggests, the Cornell artificial mouth is based more on smell than on taste.

Maybe taste is a more subjective sensation than those detected by the other senses. That could explain why the artificial replication of taste seems to be taking longer than that of the other senses. Another reason could be that the expected commercial applications for a tasting machine are presumed to be less lucrative than those for other artificial senses, and therefore that less money has been spent on developing artificial taste than for the other senses. Whatever the reason for it, artificial taste remains the least commercially developed of the artificial senses.

The five senses may be at various stages of being replicated by machines, but an artificial brain will probably take longer to develop than any of the senses.

According to the technology road map of British Telecom, the artificial brain is over three decades away. On the face of it, that is surprising. Supercomputers capable of processing a thousand billion instructions per second are on the market, and the capability to build even more powerful computers is not only growing fast but is actually accelerating.

When it comes to simulating complicated models like the worldwide weather, or a nuclear explosion, or the behaviour of the oceans, or an economy, or DNA, or seismic data, or airflow around engines, or oil extraction, a supercomputer can do the job quicker than several million of the best human brains. But when it comes to recognising or creating emotion, humour, intuition, imagination or images, the dimmest human individual is more capable than the most powerful supercomputer.

The main problem for computers is lateral thinking. Computers are built to perform their tasks sequentially. Even where one computer has many processors it doesn't produce lateral processing—just many separate streams of sequential processing.

That's why projects which are attempting to build artificial human-type brains—like the Zurich-based Institute of Neuro-informatics—go for a different type of basic building block than that which is used in conventional supercomputers.

Whereas supercomputer builders use microprocessor chips and memory chips, brain builders use a type of chip structure called a 'neural network'. A neural network chip does not have much processing power, but it has a lot of connections to other neural network chips. In that respect it is very like the neuron cells which make up the brain.

It is possible that it is the highly connected structure of neurons that enables humans to make creative leaps of imagination and logic based on connecting facts and thoughts, observations and intuitions, that haven't been connected before.

The Institute of Neuro-informatics wants to attach an eye to its brain and give it a motor to move around so it can learn visually from its environment.

Although, according to British Telecom's thinking, it will be the year 2035 before a complete example of such a brain can be built, BT is saying that artificial brain cells will be available by 2017, and artificial brain implants by 2025.

With serious research and commercial establishments around the world working on artificial versions of the five senses and the brain, if BT is right it can be expected that results will start with artificial ears in the year 2000.

As is the way of technology products, long before silicon senses are perfected, imperfect versions will be marketed. For instance, PC-based videoconferencing products of today show jerky, poor images but dedicated videoconferencing studios show TV-quality pictures. Gradually all videoconferencing will be of TV quality.

In the same way we can expect, at first, to see widely differing models of ears, mouths, eyes, skin, and noses appearing on the market, followed by an overall general level of improvement.

What it will all mean for human lifestyle when tied into the computing and communicating infrastructures that we have now, and will have later, is awe-inspiring. There will be no terrestrial limit to what we can see, hear, taste, smell or touch, or where we can transfer our thoughts and feelings.

The new products of the 21st century should make the major inventions of the 20th century—TV, jet planes, computers—seem like kids' toys.

TV made mass populations aware of different places and cultures. Jet planes allowed people to visit them cheaply. The commercialisation of the two technologies had the most far-reaching effects on mass understanding. Furthermore as the products of those technologies declined rapidly in price they became affordable to ordinary citizens in the developed world, giving them lifestyles previously only lived by the wealthy few.

In the same way, the technological developments of the 21st century will give people powers only previously bestowed, in mythology, on gods.

That's because, when the senses and the brain can be manufactured artificially, and when the world's communications networks are optical—all of which could happen within the next 100 years—then humans are going to acquire physical capabilities that defy geographical and physical limitations.

With senses and brains that can plug into the world's communications networks and with networks of virtually infinite power, people will be able to pick up any information, sensation, image, sound, smell or taste from anywhere on the planet, instantly, wherever they happen to be.

And obviously the corollary is true—anyone will be able to send any thought, sight, sound, message, taste, smell or sensation they experience to anyone else on Earth wherever they are.

The sensations of rounding Cape Horn, sitting on the top of Mount Everest, scuba diving on Australia's Great Barrier Reef, walking along the Great Wall of China or riding a camel in the Sahara Desert under a full moon could be experienced between waking and getting out of bed.

Of course this all depends on people wanting to have chips implanted in their brains. Implants such as heart pace-makers and chips for hearing have been accepted, but people could be very resistant to the idea of brain chips with all the implications for thought control.

Clearly it would be an advantage to the leaders of groups of people such as employees of a company, or members of a religious sect, to have all their members carrying a chip which could deliver information, objectives and instructions and send back reports.

Whether to have the implant could prove to be a severe test of loyalties for the company employee of the future. For fanatical sects, however, the power such implants would give them to coordinate their strategies would be quite alarming.

The question is already being asked—what will governments do with the technology? Obviously just a simple body implant, like tagging an animal, would make it very simple for governments to track their citizens' whereabouts using the satellites of the global positioning system (GPS).

That possibility has already roused concern, but if, instead of a body implant, it was a brain implant, then the implications are much more far-reaching—governments would not only know where citizens were going but could tell them where to go.

These are all questions which will loom for future legislators, but maybe not that far into the future—British Telecom is talking about implants being possible within 30 years.

If BT is right in its prediction that an artificial brain will be built by 2035, the question will then loom of quite what we would do with artificial brains.

Nowadays the contents of a computer are quite simply transferred to another computer. It seems possible that when we're sufficiently advanced to build a brain, we'll also be sufficiently advanced to download the contents of a brain. If we could download the contents of a brain, we could copy them, add or subtract them, or transfer them to another brain—either an artificial one or even another human brain.

People could swap brains. Two nomads on different sides of the planet could simply pipe the contents of their brains to each other down an optical cable and set out to explore their neighbourhood in a different body—just as people house-swap nowadays for their holidays.

Or artificial brains on artificial bodies could be kept by rental agencies and you could pipe your brain into an artificial humanoid or cyborg and explore the neighbourhood that way, rather like renting a car when you get to an airport. This could hit the airline business badly.

With the contents of brains copyable and transferable, it might become possible to buy copies of the contents of particularly fine brains and keep them in a brain collection just as we keep books and CDs. Every now and again we could take out a brain and plug into it when we want enlightenment, advice or information.

It would be a good test of a politician's integrity. If they wanted to tell us their thoughts, instead of making speeches they could have copies of their brains distributed and we could see exactly what they're thinking. Unfortunately it would probably not be long before politicians found ways of sanitising the contents of their copied brains—just as they sanitise their speeches.

It might seem to us, today, that it would be an interesting experience to get inside someone else's brain and think their thoughts—it could become a consumer craze in the 21st century. But one wonders how soon the novelty would wear off. Few people's thoughts are unfailingly or unendingly interesting.

But think of the public demand for copies of pop stars' brains or even criminals' brains—it being debatable whether public taste will improve in the next 100 years.

The big issue associated with artificial brains and their ability to hold the contents of a human brain is the issue of immortality.

If the contents of a human brain can be downloaded and stored in an artificial brain, then there's no reason for the contents of anyone's brain to be lost.

It could happen—and maybe not that far in the future—that people will have to confront the question: do I want the contents of my brain to live forever?

Judging by the number of people who pay to be frozen and kept in suspended animation hoping to be thawed out and revived by a subsequent generation, there will be some people who will take the option of having the contents of their brains transferred into artificial brains.

And since transferring into an artificial brain does not rely on the chance of a future generation deciding to thaw you out, it seems possible that more people could take up the offer of transferring the contents of their brains into artificial brains. This might be especially attractive if you could talk to friends who now inhabited an artificial brain—maybe sitting in the head of a 'cyborg' or a humanised type of robot. If these friends vouched for the pleasures of the brain transfer—no more headaches, no more grocery bills, no more doctor's fees—then many people might take up the opportunity to go humanoid.

Fanciful? If 200 years ago someone had said that within a few generations it would be possible to see people walking and talking after they are dead, he would have been thought crazy. But film made it possible. It's the same with TV. People 100 years ago would never have believed that you would be able to see and hear someone if they were on the other side of the world. Even 50 years ago people would have thought you crazy if you had said that several hundred million people would own computers in 50 years' time. But they do.

Technology has a track record of turning the unimaginable into reality, and it will again. In as short a time span as a couple of generations, one of the greatest prizes ever sought by mankind—the ability to live forever—could be won.

The astonishing thing is that we are now seeing ways, and are exploring technologies, which make immortality possible. Even if it takes four more generations to get there, that would still make the 21st century one to remember.

Certainly if popular culture is any judge—and science fiction has often become science fact—then the world of the cyborg and the humanoid is not far away. Books and films on the subject of man-made people abound. Many children probably believe that the technology already exists.

Achieving immortality could end up being one of those great events in technology history which turns out to be a yawn because everyone expected it anyway.

The reason why it has been so extensively trailed in the popular media and is so widely taken for granted is probably because the progress towards artificial senses and brains is an evolutionary one, coming bit by bit.

It's always the whizz-bang inventions that no one expected and which can be popularised cheaply that capture the public imagination—like steam trains, transistor radios or gramophones. When new inventions are commercialised slowly, like the introduction of the telephone, they stir little public enthusiasm.

Having transferable, immortal brains may be a very big trick for technology to pull off, but the public reaction to it is unknowable. There is no doubt that it would cause all sorts of interesting problems. How do you catch a criminal as he flits from inhabiting one cyborg to another? What would you do if a brain became irredeemably evil? Does a disembodied brain have citizens' rights? We can all think of thousands of such thorny issues.

Logically one would expect bodies to become redundant. After all, if every possible kind of stimulation, entertainment and information can be piped direct into your brain, then what's the point of having a body?

You want to walk round your garden? The exact sensations of walking round your garden—the mud, the thorns, the rain, etc.— can all be transmitted straight to your brain which, because all sensations are experienced via electrical signals to the brain, is the only place you're going to experience walking around your garden anyway.

In that case, people might think, what's the point of a body? It only goes wrong giving you pain. Or it ages. Or it makes demands—for food, drink and so on. With all thought and feeling simply a stream of electrical signals to the brain, people could decide that bodies are redundant.

It would be a strange destiny for the human race if it turned into billions of brains stacked, immobile, in darkened rooms experiencing all the pleasures and sensations of a Sultan. It might solve the traffic problem, but the human race could be wiped out by a power cut!

The point of these musings is that although we know how the technology is moving and how fast it evolves, and we know what applications are being developed, we can still speculate endlessly on what it will mean for the human race.

That is interesting enough in itself, but the scale of the achievements technology is about to deliver make it very important that as many people as possible are aware of what's happening and of the effects it might have.

The more people think about it, the better they may figure out the answers to the social questions raised by these technological achievements.

Because the 21st century promises to be an exciting time for the human race—freed for the first time from the constraints of geography and distance.

Liberation from long oppressions can release great energies, and we are going to be released from a ten-millennia-long oppression dictated by the need to settle in order to survive.

The enthralling story of the 21st century is going to be about what people do with their freedom.

INDEX